About the author

Sarah Ockwell-Smith is the mother of four young adult children. She has a BSc in Psychology and worked for several years in pharmaceutical research and development. Following the birth of her first child, Sarah retrained as an antenatal teacher and birth and postnatal doula. She has also undertaken training in hypnotherapy and psychotherapy. Sarah specialises in gentle parenting methods. Sarah is also the tween and teen expert for the GoodtoKnow website.

Sarah is the author of fourteen other parenting books: *BabyCalm, ToddlerCalm, The Gentle Sleep Book, The Gentle Parenting Book, Why Your Baby's Sleep Matters, The Gentle Discipline Book, The Gentle Potty Training Book, The Gentle Eating Book, The Second Baby Book, The Starting School Book, Between, How to Be a Calm Parent, Beginnings* and *Because I Said So*. She frequently writes for magazines and newspapers, and is often called upon as a parenting expert for national television and radio.

HOW TO
RAISE
A
TEEN

SARAH OCKWELL-SMITH

PIATKUS

PIATKUS

First published in Great Britain in 2024 by Piatkus

1 3 5 7 9 10 8 6 4 2

A CIP catalogue record for this book
is available from the British Library.

ISBN: 978-0349-43647-0

Typeset in Stone Serif by M Rules
Illustration by Rodney Paull
Printed and bound in Great Britain by Clays Ltd, Elcograf S.p.A.

Papers used by Piatkus are from well-managed forests
and other responsible sources.

Piatkus
An imprint of
Little, Brown Book Group
Carmelite House
50 Victoria Embankment
London EC4Y 0DZ

An Hachette UK Company
www.hachette.co.uk

www.littlebrown.co.uk

Contents

Introduction

It was the spring of 1992. John Major's Conservative Party had just won a second term in the UK's general election, Disneyland Paris had just opened, George Michael wowed millions when he performed on stage with Queen at the Freddie Mercury tribute concert at Wembley Stadium, Kate Moss had just posed topless with Mark Wahlberg for a Calvin Klein advert and *Beverly Hills, 90210* was the most talked about show on TV.

I was sixteen, just about to take my GCSE exams, struggling with anxiety and low self-esteem and trying to work out who I was and what I wanted to be in a family who had already decided for me. I was a talented artist and wanted to study fine art at a college in London. My parents, however, were concerned that this wasn't an appropriate career choice, and it was decided, with little input from me, that art should instead remain a hobby and I would move from my state high school to take my A-levels at a local private school. My artistic skills had won me an art scholarship, making it affordable for my parents who had grown up in large families with little money in the East End of London and left school with only a handful of O-levels between them. It was a dream for them to have a child at such a prestigious school. It wasn't my dream, though my dream didn't matter, because I was young and naïve about 'the real world'.

My nickname during this period was 'Stroppy Sarah'. Still, I was a 'good girl'. I rarely rebelled, broke curfews or answered back. I did my homework and begrudgingly completed my chores. I also spent hours alone in my bedroom, decorated with black and white Athena posters, sulking after disagreements with my parents. I can vividly remember desperately wanting them to come to my room and say, 'It's hard being a teen. How can I help?' But they never did. Instead, I spent hours sulking and brooding, trying to find a sense of belonging in a world full of people who I felt didn't understand me. 'Stroppy Sarah' thought *she* was the problem, or at least her hormones (something else her emotionally erratic behaviour was frequently blamed on) and her age were. Nobody told her anything different. It took years for her to develop self-confidence and to pursue her own path in life, one that led to writing rather than art – but still, a creative career that teen Sarah would likely have been steered away from.

Why am I telling you all this? Because it's so important that we remember how we felt as teenagers ourselves if we want to truly understand the teenagers in our lives today.

I'd like you to take a pause from reading this book for a moment to revisit your own adolescence. Try to think of a time between the ages of thirteen and twenty-one, when you felt similarly misunderstood or unsupported by your parents or carers. Take a piece of paper or use your electronic device and write a few sentences about what was happening at that time in your world. How were you feeling? How were you behaving? What did you hope your parents or carers would say to you? What did they actually say or do? Keep these words safe, because I'd like you to refer back to them later in this book. For now, however, just acknowledge that there were always underlying feelings beneath your so-called problematic behaviour as a teen, and often they revolved around not being understood or supported by those closest to you. Sadly, we forget all too quickly, but revisiting your own past feelings is key to deciphering those of your teen today.

We often paint teenagers in a negative light. We call them

rude, disrespectful, manipulative, stubborn and deliberately defiant. We are wrong. We have all been teenagers; we know how
misunderstood we felt. We know that any time we said, or did,
something that could be construed as disrespectful there was an
unmet need, or problem driving our behaviour. We all felt, at
times, disrespected by adults. We all vowed, at some point, that
we wouldn't be like them if we ever had children in the future . . .
and yet here we are. Teenagers today get as much short shrift as
we did in our own teen years. Nothing has changed, except we
are now the adults, and we have, indeed, become the grown-ups
we swore we never would.

Society has a funny way of perpetuating distrust and disdain
towards teenagers. This is nothing new, with frequent protestations about the state of 'the youth of today' and how teen
behaviour is apparently worse than ever (a myth we will bust
later in this book). Teenagers have always been the butt of jokes
and the cause of many complaints from adults, and I suspect
they always will be. My hope with this book, however, is to try
to change things a little. I want to help readers, including you,
not only to see how magical their teens are (or the teens that
they teach or care for) but to understand them a little more, to
make things easier and happier for all.

Am I suggesting that teenagers are always right and adults are
always wrong? Absolutely not. Teens often do, and say, stupid
things – indeed, I expect this is part of the reason why you're
reading this book – and raising them is often infuriating and
exhausting. They make mistakes, they get angry, they get into
trouble, they can be lazy, rude, obstinate and argumentative. I'm
not making excuses for any of these behaviours or saying that
they are OK. What I am saying, is that the best way through
these years is to work *with* your teens, to support them, guide
them and to understand them, rather than working *against* them,
as so much parenting advice suggests. The easiest and most rewarding path through these years is one you walk together with

your teen, with as much emphasis on your own behaviour as on theirs. After all, every descriptor I used near the start of this paragraph can also explain common adult behaviours – and if we're not perfect, why should we expect our teens to be?

Who is this book for?

My career as an author and parenting coach started two decades ago, with parents of babies and toddlers. It quickly became apparent to me, that there was a flood of information out there for parents and carers relating to the first three years. There were a myriad of activity classes, support groups, public-health information, websites, influencer accounts and online discussion groups aimed at understanding child development from birth through to early school age, and so many books (including my own)! After this, however, it seemed that the information and support shrank ever more with each year of increasing age of the child.

In early 2021, I decided to write about 'tweenagers' – children between the ages of eight and thirteen. My book *Between* was met with many proclamations of relief, with thousands of parents telling me they were so glad that finally information about this age group was available. They told me they felt like there was a scarcity of information and support once children entered the tween years. But if the information about tweenagers is scarce, it is pretty much non-existent when it comes to teens and young adults, and yet their parents feel they need more information than ever as they struggle to understand and raise them. It seems unjust that at the period of most need for information and support parents are faced with the least.

My aim with this book is to try to meet that need. My own four children are now leaving their teen years, and these pages contain all the information I wish I'd had from the beginning.

Ultimately, this book is for anybody who has an interest in understanding thirteen- to twenty-one-year-olds, whether that's parents, carers, teachers, therapists and counsellors, health professionals or anybody else who works with teens or their parents.

Why thirteen to twenty-one?

If the teen years run from thirteen to nineteen, why have I included twenty- and twenty-one-year-olds in this book? Similarly, if children are legally adults at the age of eighteen, why haven't I stopped there?

Because, from my own experience, and that of parents I have spoken to, children (who may now technically be adults) don't stop needing you, or having problems, the second they grow out of being a teenager. That doesn't mean the same isn't true when they reach twenty-one, of course, however things are usually easier by then.

Another reason why I have continued this book until twenty-one is because this is the age when most (who choose to go) graduate from university, and this time of life brings unique challenges to parents and carers, some of which I will be covering here.

What will you find in this book?

This book is made up of eleven chapters. We start with the concept of 'holding on' to your teen in Chapter 1, when we discuss some of the most common worries experienced by parents and carers at this age, and actions and beliefs that can damage the relationship with teens. The teen years seem to be a constant tussle between holding on and letting go, and this chapter helps parents and carers to strike a healthy balance for both themselves and their teens. In Chapter 2 we look at some of the common causes of difficult behaviour and conflict during this period of parenting through the lens of the development and capabilities of the teenage brain and its impact on behaviour.

Chapter 3 takes a look at the inner thoughts and feelings of teenagers, considering their changing identities and sense of self as they grow. We will talk about a young person's drive for a sense of belonging and how to support their developing identity. In Chapter 4 we go a little deeper into the teen psyche and consider the concepts of self-confidence and self-esteem, questioning how these develop and how parents and carers play a role. We will also consider how we, as adults, can help teens to grow into young adults with good mental health.

Chapter 5 looks at discipline and some of the difficult behaviour that is common during adolescence, discussing how parents and carers can work through these difficulties with their teens and young adults. In this chapter we also consider the importance of setting and enforcing boundaries. Chapter 6 takes a journey outside of the home and discusses issues at school, including homework, exams, behaviour at school and common education-related struggles faced by parents of teens. Chapter 7 discusses how teens use screens and the internet, and what every parent and carer needs to know to keep these safe and ensure that they remain a useful and not damaging part of their teen's everyday life. This chapter also discusses alcohol, drugs and vaping – three areas that most parents of teens will have to tackle at some point. Chapter 8 concerns relationships, starting with a look at friendships and sibling relationships, how these change throughout the teen years and how to help your young person cope with common difficulties. We also look at romantic relationships and how to guide your teen through their first sexual experiences (because no matter how uncomfortable you may feel, they *will* have them).

Chapter 9 focuses on increasing independence, including

learning to drive, and having an eye on the future, with discussions of 'next steps' concerning education and work, and helping your teen to decide on a career path. Chapter 10 is all about 'letting go', learning to unfold your wings and encouraging your (now) young adult to fly, while also considering your new place in the world with your empty nest. Raising teenagers is as much about raising yourself for the next chapter in your own life as it is raising your child for theirs. Finally, Chapter 11 comprises some questions I am frequently asked by parents and carers of teens and young adults. It's hard to answer every specific query that readers may have, but I'm hopeful that this chapter will go some way towards that. I've worked with parents for a long time now and receive the same questions repeatedly, so I've included the most common ones in this chapter.

Why have I not divided this book into age-related chapters?

The teen years are not easily isolated into little bite-size information chunks based upon age. Everything is relevant, everything is interrelated. For this reason, I would suggest that you read all chapters, even if your child is only just thirteen.

Considering the future is of utmost importance when thinking about how you want to raise your child today. If you're reading as the parent or carer of an eleven- or twelve-year-old, keen to prepare for what lies ahead, you may find some sections that are not immediately pertinent to your life today; however, I firmly believe that you can't have too much knowledge, even if you store it away somewhere safe for the next few years. Similarly, it's never too late to read this book, so if you're reading this as the parent or carer of a twenty-year-old, know that every chapter applies to you, too, because there is no magical change that occurs at this age. At twenty-one, your young person still has several years of brain development left ahead of them and their behaviour is far more similar to that of a teenager than a fully mature adult.

A quick note on terminology

You'll notice I have used several different terms throughout this introduction: teens, children, young adults and teenagers. None of these feels quite right to me. 'Teens' and 'teenagers' exclude twenty- and twenty-one-year-olds, while 'children' doesn't feel right considering they are legally adults at eighteen. 'Young adults' on the other hand feels a little too mature for those who are just on the cusp of the teen years. For this reason, from this point on I will use the term 'young person' to refer to those aged thirteen to twenty-one. Not only do I personally find this term the most fitting, but I also feel that referring to them as 'a person' is important when it comes to reminding ourselves that young people have feelings, needs and rights, just like us – something that is very important in a society that seemingly seeks to de-personalise the experience of teens and young adults today.

I hope this introduction has piqued your interest and that the issues in the chapter descriptions cover the topics and concerns you may have. Whenever I write a book for parents and carers, my goal is not to be the 'all-knowing' expert imparting advice and keeping you reliant on me for more in the future; rather, my aim is to help you realise that you are already the expert on your own young person and their needs, and to help you see that you know much more than you think you do.

Ready to delve in? Let's go!

Chapter 1

Holding On

Isn't it funny how day by day nothing changes, but when you look back everything is different.

C. S. Lewis, author

Toing and froing, back and forth, push and pull – these all perfectly describe the bittersweet dichotomy that characterises the teen years and early twenties. These are the years in which your young person veers wildly between wanting to be big – an independent 'grown-up' – versus wanting to be little and needing you just as much as they did when they were a young child. The constant flip-flopping of needs is not only difficult for young people to assimilate, but is often emotionally draining for parents, too. Is today going to be a 'holding-on' or a 'letting-go' kind of day? Will your young person want hugs and to revel in your care, or will they want to stand completely independent of you, shrugging off attempts from you to hold their hand, both literally and metaphorically?

These years are a confusing dance, where both partners are unsure of the routine. Sometimes you waltz elegantly, perfectly in step with each other, while at others you can barely move for stepping on one another's toes, angry that neither of you knows the moves. As your young person leaves childhood behind, this is a period of mourning and confusion for you both, mixed with fizzing excitement for the future and plenty of doubt and frustration. Now is not a time to let go fully, though. Your young person needs you just as much now as they ever did, perhaps even more so. What they need from you, however, looks different to the parenting of previous years, which is where the confusion sets in for many parents and carers.

What *do* they need? They need you to guide and support them and, most importantly, they need you to hold on to them while preparing to let go in the not-too-distant future. If that (understandably) sounds confusing, the easiest way to make sense of how to hold on while letting go is to rewind the clock to infancy and the attachment that you built with your then baby. Let's do a quick recap.

Attachment and young people

Attachment relates to the ability of a child (and here I do mean child, not young person) to seek and receive reassurance and support from a nurturing caregiver when they feel scared or anxious. A strong attachment occurs when the caregiver is ready and willing to support the child to manage their emotions and to provide a 'secure base' for them to return to for reassurance whenever they encounter something in the world that makes them feel scared or nervous. In infancy, this attachment is not only emotional, but physical, too. All parents know the desperate cries of a ten-month-old baby clinging on to them for dear life in the middle of the night, refusing to be put back in their crib. This clinginess actually indicates a job well done – a parent who has created a strong attachment with their baby. This drive to maintain physical proximity and trust that their primary caregiver will meet their needs with consistency is what helps infants to develop and explore the world around them. When that ten-month-old 'clingy' baby feels secure in the knowledge that their caregiver will always be there when they need them, they develop the confidence to explore and take the first steps towards independence.

It is these normal, everyday interactions with their parents that teach young children about relationships with other people, too. If they are raised with a secure attachment to their caregiver, the growing child will develop certain expectations of interactions with others, believing that other adults they meet will be willing and able to support them physically and psychologically, too. As children grow, so does the number of important attachment figures in their lives, taking in wider family members, childcare workers, teachers and other caregivers.

While we may have been talking about babies and young children over the last couple of paragraphs, these attachment roles are necessary as children grow into teens. It may feel as if you are less and less needed as a secure base these days and you may question your attachment to your young person, but in the teen years, attachment takes a more psychological than physical form. Your young person still needs you just as much as they did when they were a wailing ten-month-old in your arms, they just hide it pretty well. Indeed, it is often in the moments when they are acting in the most unlikeable of ways and pushing you away that the need to reinforce attachment and the feeling of security and regulation that it brings for them is at its highest.

While holding on in the teen years can be difficult, so is beginning to let go, and both have a role in attachment. We can often resist encouraging independence with our young people, when we wrestle with thoughts about safety and trust, and especially at times when it feels as if we are losing control of them. Boundaries are, of course, important during these years (something we will talk about more in Chapter 5) but trying to control too much inhibits a young person's feelings of trust and security and will inevitably backfire. The key to attachment at this age is to find a balance, letting go just enough that the bond between parent or carer and young person is strengthened and they know they can always return to your arms (metaphorically or otherwise) when they need to.

The emphasis of attachment in these years should be on letting go physically but holding on emotionally. Sadly, however, many parents of teens are so focused on controlling their young person's actions that they unknowingly damage the emotional connection. Holding on to that emotional attachment is arguably the most important thing a parent can do during these years. Your arms may be empty now your young person is no longer a baby, but your hearts and souls should be connected just as much as before, because it is this connection that will help you both not only to survive but also to thrive through these years.

What does secure attachment look like in teens?

Assessment of attachment in infancy focuses heavily on the baby's reactions when their parent leaves them temporarily and when they are reunited. Naturally, it is hard to ask a baby what attachment means to them and how the presence or absence of their parent or carer makes them feel, so it is inferred by observations of their behaviour. As children get older, we have the benefit of being able to ask them how they feel. Research shows that in adolescence, trust from a young person that their parent or carer will be available for them when they need them is a key marker of a secure attachment.[1] However, trust is something that erodes quickly throughout the teen years.

As relationships with peers become increasingly influential, a young person's attachment with their parent or carer may appear to take more of a back seat, but it is still just as important as it was in infancy. While many parents may feel that their influence over their young person diminishes and that these years are shaped more by their peers, research indicates that the attachment with parents or carers is still key to a young person's emotional and social development.[2] It has also been shown that a strong attachment with a parent or carer during adolescence correlates with better mental health.[3] Young people with strong attachments to their parents are happier, less stressed, have better self-esteem and emotional intelligence; they are also more able to communicate their own feelings and to understand and communicate with others and have more positive social relationships. In short, parents are always influential, even when they don't feel they are.

What do young people want from their parents and carers?

While writing this book I surveyed a hundred young people, aged between thirteen and twenty-one, and asked them what they valued most about their parents. More than 70 per cent of their responses mentioned parental support, trust, love and guidance. Here is a selection of their responses to the question 'What's the best thing about your parent(s)?'

- 'They love me even when I do bad things.'
- 'They are caring, but not controlling.'
- 'I know they are always there for me.'
- 'They are always around to support me.'
- 'They aren't judgemental.'
- 'They listen to me.'
- 'Being able to talk to my mum.'
- 'Their willingness to help me.'

- 'I can talk to them about anything.'
- 'They trust me.'
- 'I know there is always one person who will stand up for me.'
- 'I get to be myself with them.'

Raising young people can feel like a thankless task at times. Gone are the overenthusiastic expressions of love scrawled on homemade cards, the sticky toddler kisses and smiling coos from a baby. Often, they are replaced by shaking away your hand as you reach for theirs or dismissive grunts in response to your 'I love you'. When the superficial teen behaviour is stripped back, however, they are just as much in need of your love, acceptance and attachment as they ever were.

Attachment instinct: when young people learn who they can trust

While babies and toddlers may have an instinct about which adults feel most comfortable to them, as children get older and reach adolescence their logical and rational thinking skills develop (something we will discuss more in the next chapter) and they can begin to analyse and hypothesise about which adults can meet their needs for attachment and help them to feel supported and secure. They can also make informed judgements about the opposite and begin to learn which adults cannot meet their emotional support needs.

When a young person is feeling dysregulated emotionally and unable to cope with a situation they find themselves in, they naturally reach out to those they feel most attached to, usually their parent. If, however, the parent is preoccupied (be that with work, financial or relationship worries, or something else) or they are inconsistent with their responses, it can leave the young person feeling let down and unsupported. In this case, their behaviour often worsens, because not only are they lacking in guidance, they are also struggling with the feeling that they are not as securely attached to the adult as they'd believed. This combination often results in behaviour that is described as 'out of control' or 'acting out', which fractures the relationship with the parent even more.

Unfortunately, this is a cycle that many young people find themselves in, especially those exhibiting the most difficult behaviours. The young person is blamed for their poor choices, they find themselves on the receiving end of punishments and admonishment when what they really need is connection and somebody to listen, trust and support them. Attachment is the key to solving almost all issues that occur in the teen years (and beyond).

As young people grow, they begin to develop new attachment figures, including peers and romantic partners. These new attachments can cause them to re-evaluate their childhood attachments and draw their attention to any problems with them, leading them to doubt their parents and carers and drive a further wedge into those relationships. If the young person feels that the new attachment figures are more trustworthy than their parent, they may reach out to them in times of need, pushing their parent away. So begins the cycle of young people who are influenced more by their peers than their parents, and who choose to seek advice and support outside of the home. This is something that many parents complain about, but don't fully understand that usually it is their own actions that cause this phenomenon.

Does this mean that if you went through a period of not being emotionally available, you have damaged your relationship with your young person forever? Absolutely not. You can start to be more reliable and available today. The best thing about having an older child is that you can talk to them, and they understand far more about the complexities of adult life. It's never too late to start working on your relationship with your young person. Similarly, an attachment figure doesn't always have to be you; it can be another trusted adult close to your young person. Research shows that when young people have a trustworthy adult (who is not their parent/carer) in their lives from whom they feel comfortable seeking reassurance, it can help them to feel more settled.[4] If, for whatever reason, you are struggling at the moment to connect to your young person, can you think of another adult who could take on this role? Albeit temporarily. A relative? A family friend? Helping your young person to build connections with other trusted adults can give you much-needed breathing space while you work to be able to be fully accessible yourself.

Why most common teen parenting advice damages attachments

Take a look at any internet parenting discussion group and you'll quickly come across a parent struggling with their young person's behaviour. They will be flooded with replies saying, 'They have to learn; you have to teach them a lesson', 'There have to be consequences to their behaviour', 'I wouldn't let mine get away with that; they'd get their Xbox taken away if they tried' and 'They need a good punishment'. Almost all common parenting advice today, especially for the teen years, focuses on punishment for bad behaviour by taking something away from the young person, ranging from screen time to their freedom, with 'grounding' still a common choice. Exclusion of some form is also popular, especially sending young people to their room or banishing them from fun family activities. While these techniques may initially produce short-term compliance (provided the young person is sufficiently scared by the punishment or unhappy about the exclusion), in the long term they are problematic because they create detachment.

Through common discipline methods we teach young people that they cannot rely on us for support when they are struggling to control their emotions. We teach them that they are only worthy of our love when they are well behaved and that their connection with us only matters when they are 'good'. These approaches tell our young people that our attachment is conditional; they learn that we are not the secure, dependable, trustworthy base that they thought we were and, in time, they come to us less and less with their problems, as their orbit shifts to a new support network, populated largely by their peers.

Simply, if we want to remain the major influence in our young people's lives and we want them to know that they can always come to us for help, we cannot use discipline techniques that centre on pushing them away. Instead, we need to prioritise connection over correction.

Staying attached, even when it feels hard

We spend a lot of time in the first decade of being a parent wondering when our children will need us less intensely, longing for the time when they become independent. Then, as quick as a flash, we realise that we are living through 'the lasts' daily: the last goodnight kiss, the last bedtime story, the last piggyback, the last time we brush their hair or lay out their clothes for the day, the last time they curl up in our laps, the last time we carry them in from the car asleep and place them gently in their bed, and the last time they sneak into our beds for hugs at night.

Acknowledging 'the lasts' can sometimes leave us feeling wistful and sad as parents, making us wish that we had paid more attention and spent more time together; they can be especially hard to take alongside a young person who does not seem to connect with us in the present.

It is a young person's job to need their parents less, to test the relationship and how far they can push the boundaries. As parents, it is vital that we don't take these actions personally. Focusing on 'the lasts' and lamenting lost time and possibilities doesn't change the past and can put wedges in the present. The teen and young-adult years are all about parents and carers learning not to take things personally, and are a time when we need to be careful to not misinterpret difficult behaviour. Staying attached as children grow means living in the present and being careful to not react to our young people based on something that triggers us from our own teen years.

As our children grow, so we need to grow, too, allowing them both the space and the secure base that they need. What do they need most from us? They need parents are caregivers who are:

- Trustworthy (and who trust them)
- Consistent
- Supportive
- Encouraging (but not pushy)
- Understanding
- Good communicators
- Calm
- Non-judgemental
- Accepting

The latter three points are often the hardest. It can be so difficult to watch your young person make choices that you wouldn't, or were punished for, at a similar age, but research shows that adolescents whose parents are more critical of them are less likely to have a secure attachment.[5]

What to do when it's hard to 'be the adult'

I often say that raising teens is harder than raising younger children. Physically, things are easier, but emotionally it is far more demanding. Little kids have little issues, while big kids have much bigger issues, and young people demand a lot more parental headspace than they did a decade or so earlier. These years involve almost reparenting yourself, requiring you to do a lot of navel-gazing to unpick your triggers and learn to control your own emotions in a quest to help your young person control theirs.

One of the most important self-improvement lessons that parents of young people need to grasp is the idea of 'being the adult'. By this I mean accepting that as fully grown and experienced adults, they have more developed brains and a lot more life wisdom under their belts. When faced with difficult scenarios with an emotional young person, it is parents and carers who need to step up and be the adults in the situation; this means staying calm, taking a deep breath and focusing on attachment, support and guidance, offering the security, consistency and reliability that the young person needs. When parents do this, young people feel safe to share their concerns, which, in turn, will help them to resolve any issues and remove the difficult behaviour that is a symptom of the problem.

Being the adult is hard, though. Nobody is perfect and we all make mistakes. This is a point we will come back to repeatedly throughout this book. Although the ideal would be for you to be the adult 100 per cent of the time, I understand (as a parent of young people myself) that's not humanly possible. Life gets in the way. We become 'full up' with the concerns and worries of adulthood. We get tired and, as hard as we try, we will often act out just as much as our young people.

So what do we do in these difficult times?

- You have to start with giving yourself grace and recognising what you bring to the parenting table – years of conditioned behaviours aren't going to be undone overnight. If you were raised by parents who yelled, punished or shamed you as a teen, then reflexively you will tend to be this way with your own young people. It takes time to overcome these deeply embedded instinctual behaviours.
- You have to try to make some space. It's hard to be sensitive to your young person's emotional needs and distress if you are 'full up' yourself. This looks different for everybody, but it could involve saying 'no' more if you are inclined to jump in and take on too many tasks, having better boundaries with others and looking at what doesn't serve you in your life any more.
- You need to try not to discipline when you're angry or react to your young person's superficial words or actions. Yes, sometimes their words are cutting and make you see red mist, but, ultimately, they are just words and they are indicative of a young person who is struggling and needs you to see beyond what they say and look for the deeper cause of their dysregulated behaviour. Take a breath, remind yourself 'I'm the adult; I don't have to react to this' and wait until things are a little calmer before deciding on an action plan.
- When (note, I haven't said 'if' because it *will* happen) you slip up and forget or you don't manage to be the adult, know that you can always make things right afterwards by apologising to your young person. Let them know that you are sorry that you couldn't be

the adult they needed in the moment, but that you've had time to calm down and now you're ready to help. Psychologists call this 'rupture and repair' – with your apology you are repairing the temporary rupture of your attachment with your young person, while also teaching them how to apologise to others when they mess up.

- Drop the guilt. Nobody gets parenting right all the time, especially not raising teens. There is no point dwelling on your past actions, whether that's times when you utilised discipline techniques that focused on detachment or when you now realise you were most definitely not the adult. This retrospective self-admonishment doesn't help anybody, least of all your young person. When you know better, you do better, but even when you know better there are still going to be times when you don't quite manage to put that knowledge into action. Learn from your mistakes, resolve to start afresh tomorrow and look forwards, not back. Regret doesn't produce change, only action does.

Being the adult is hard work, but it is what we need to do if we want to navigate these years with as much ease as possible, while retaining a close bond with our young people. Holding on again requires an element of stepping back: this time it is our triggers, anger and frustration we need to let go of in order to stay close to our young people.

Can you be too attached to your young person?

A common concern I come across when I'm talking about attachment with parents is the idea of being 'too attached'.

The media like to label parents who are strongly attached to their young person and actively involved in their lives, calling them 'helicopter' or 'snowplough' parents. Helicopter parents hover over their young person, constantly involving themselves in their life, leaving little space for them to increase their orbit away from them and to learn independently. Snowplough parents metaphorically stand in front of their young person, dealing with anything life throws at them, ploughing a clear path, free of challenges and obstacles. Clearly, while helicopter and snowplough parents are well intentioned, they haven't managed to strike a balance between holding on and letting go, and this clips the wings of their young person.

The type of attachment I am advocating is more akin to scaffolding. Parents who scaffold their young people create a framework to help hold and build them up; the support is there when needed, but the parents are mindful to make space and remove the scaffolding as their young people become more confident in tackling life alone. Parents who scaffold are mindful of attachment, but don't want their young people to become overly reliant on them. Rather, they want to create confident and secure individuals, while also letting them know that they can always reach out for more support if they ever feel wobbly.

Time is precious

Perhaps you've seen the popular social media video or meme that proclaims, 'You only have eighteen summers with your child, so make them count'? Time is indeed precious, and as young people grow, they naturally spend less time with their parents and family, dramatically so from age fifteen. According to the American Time Use Survey, fifteen-year-olds spend an average of 267 minutes per day with their family, and by age eighteen, this has fallen to 236 minutes, steadily declining from there on, reaching only 152 minutes per day by the age of twenty-one for those who still live at home.[6] This reduced time with family is replaced by time with romantic partners, colleagues or simply alone.

I think all parents of young people should be mindful of passing time and making the most of it, but not to the point that they feel guilty if they are not enjoying every second – because honestly, nobody does. It is not feasible to make every day of those eighteen summers count. While our young people may spend less time with us as they grow, this is something to celebrate, as it is indicative of their increasing independence and confidence. Instead of lamenting rapidly losing time, I think it is much healthier to focus on creating the kind of relationship with our young people that allows them to feel they can always come back to us for help, advice or just to enjoy time together as they grow.

Making time to stay connected to your young person now will help ensure that the bond between you remains strong. Here are some suggestions for how to spend more quality time with your young person:

- Family board-game nights
- Family movie nights or cinema trips
- Family escape-room visits
- Inviting their friends or partners over for snacks or a barbecue
- Weekend brunches
- Creating new family-holiday traditions
- Joining them in their favourite activities, such as gaming

I love having a house full of young people. One tradition that we followed in our family was hosting Halloween or bonfire-night get-togethers in our house for our young people and their friends. Being mindful of the passage of time (without thinking in terms of time running out) can help you to embrace more fun ways to connect with your young person that will, hopefully, last for many more years to come.

Time to revisit your past again

In the Introduction, I asked you to think of a period between the ages of thirteen and twenty-one when you felt misunderstood or unsupported by your parents or carers. Did you write something down? If you didn't, grab some paper and a pen now, or use your phone to quickly make a note. I asked you to answer four questions:

- How were you feeling?
- How were you behaving?
- What did you hope your parents or carers would say to you?
- What did they actually say or do?

Looking at what you've written, what did you really need from your parents or carers at the time? I'd wager your answer probably involves understanding, support, love, guidance and acceptance – all words heavily rooted in attachment and connection, the very topic we have discussed at length in this chapter.

Instinctively, I think we all know how to raise young people because we have all been there. We all know what it felt like to not quite have our needs for attachment and nurturance met; we all know how it feels to be misunderstood. If we take these feelings and bottle them, we will know how to treat our own young people, even if the world is screaming at us to be more disciplinarian. How we ourselves were raised impacts how we raise our own young people, but most of us were not treated with the full respect and empathy we deserved. You have the power to change this cycle. Your young person needs the same thing that you needed. It's pretty simple, really, when you look at it like that, albeit not easy to achieve, which is why there are still ten more chapters of this book to go!

Every young person needs somebody who believes in them and somebody they can trust who will always be there for them when they need them, no matter how difficult their behaviour or how cutting their words. Just because they look increasingly like a fully grown adult, it doesn't mean that they need you any less. That ten-month-old reaching out for you in the middle of the night is still there. They still need you to reassure them, guide them, love them. It may not seem like it, but their orbit is still centred on you, and you still matter the most to them, even – and especially – on days when they tell you that they hate you and wish you'd die.

You have to remember to be the adult, to keep your side of the bargain and be their secure base. Holding on to your young person means retaining an influence, as well as a strong attachment. It means being there as a safe base for your young person to return to, to get instructions from when needed, while encouraging them to branch out into the world alone. It's a learning journey for everybody. You won't always get it right, and that's OK. I'm a so-called expert and I still mess up. But the most important thing is that you try.

Let's move on from attachment now and look at something that catches a lot of parents and carers of young people out, causing many arguments and anxieties unnecessarily: incorrect expectations of their behaviour, and misunderstanding their neurological capabilities. Chapter 2 will help you to appreciate what your young person is really capable of and to understand how their brains and hormones impact their behaviour.

Chapter 2

Hormones, Brains and Behaviour

There's usually an inside story to every outside behaviour.
FRED ROGERS, television host and author

'It's their hormones!'

If you raise a concern about your young person in a group of other parents, I can guarantee that within a minute talk will turn to hormones. If your young person is male, any difficulties you have will be blamed on the fact that their body is 'swimming in testosterone'; if they are female, then their behaviour will be put down to 'oodles of oestrogen'. Apparently, testosterone makes boys aggressive, rude and 'boisterous', whereas oestrogen makes girls sulky, erratic and rude, especially when it's 'the time of the month'.

What if I told you that this isn't true?

In fact, hormones have little to do with your young person's behaviour and constantly blaming it on this does them a great disservice. Why? Because dismissing behaviour as being caused by hormones prevents parents and carers from finding – and, most importantly, working with – any underlying problems. Constant talk of hormones also tries to neatly distinguish between 'boy' and 'girl' behaviour, with countless sources offering highly gender-stereotyped advice. The truth is, regardless of what sex your young person is, what they need from you is exactly the same: support, attachment, understanding and great role modelling.

Does this mean hormones have no impact at all?

No. They do – just nowhere near as much as most people think. Similarly, the idea of a 'surge of hormones' during adolescence is misguided. Hormone levels start to change significantly at the beginning of puberty, usually between the ages of nine and eleven. So if they were really the issue, we would see an impact on behaviour far before the teen years.

There are some links between certain hormones and behaviour in adolescence, however – predominantly risk-taking behaviour. Higher levels of testosterone have been linked to an increase in this, not just in boys, but in girls, too.[1,2] Interestingly, higher levels of oestradiol (a form of oestrogen) are linked with decreased risk-taking behaviours.

Sleep, teens and hormones

Perhaps the main hormonal influence of behaviour during the teen years, though, is the impact on sleep. You've probably noticed that it's getting harder and harder to get your young person out of bed in the morning. Gone are the 6 a.m. starts you had when they were little, and now they would happily sleep away the whole morning, given the chance. Bedtime, too, is often increasingly fraught during these years, particularly when you're trying to make sure that your young person has enough sleep for school (something we will cover in detail in Chapters 6 and 7). It often feels as if young people live in a different time zone to the rest of the family, waking up as you're going to bed and sleeping when you're about to start your day. This conflicting sleep schedule is the cause of many fights between young people and their parents and carers. However, it's not all their fault – there is a very real physiological reason for their sleep patterns.

As your young person grows, their hormones influence the function of a collection of nerve cells in the brain known as the suprachiasmatic nucleus (SCN for short). The SCN is considered the pacemaker of the body's circadian rhythm, or body clock, responding to changes in light levels that occur during the day and night. During adolescence, a circadian shift occurs, known as an 'evening chronotype' (chronotype meaning the body's natural drive to sleep), whereby young people, categorised as natural night owls, have an innate leaning towards later sleep onsets at night and later wake times in the morning. Girls experience this circadian shift on average one year before boys and reach the pinnacle of sleep-onset delay and later waking by age nineteen, with boys reaching it at twenty.[3] After this point, sleep slowly changes to a more mature adult chronotype, in part due to differences in hormone regulation and also because of more mature behaviours surrounding sleep hygiene.

So the good news is that you won't always be living in a different time zone to your young person – things will change naturally given time. But the challenge lies in learning how to accommodate their evening chronotype while living in a morning-chronotype (waking early in the morning with earlier evening sleep onsets) world (more on this in Chapter 6).

Brains and behaviour

While hormones do clearly have an impact on behaviour during the teen years, when we add brain development into the picture, too, we start to understand a lot more. You see, your young person's brain, with a small influence from hormones, is responsible for almost all the behaviours you find challenging. And understanding the hormone–brain interplay is like flicking on a light bulb for parents and young people alike, identifying the root causes of almost everything that both parties struggle to cope with.

Let's take a look at some of the ways in which the young person's brain influences their behaviour.

Common complaints of parents and carers of young people

When I run workshops for parents and carers of young people, I always start by asking them to list some of their common frustrations and concerns about their young people's difficult behaviour. The following always appear – perhaps you can relate to some of them?

- Disorganisation
- Impulsivity
- Erratic emotions
- Lack of consideration for others
- Rudeness and backchat
- Not thinking about the consequences of their actions
- Being prone to procrastination
- Poor time management
- Inability to prioritise

- Irrational behaviour
- Short-term thinking (too focused on the moment, not the future)
- Overuse of their phones, gaming consoles and other screens

If you think back to your own teen years, I'd wager that you could probably tick quite a few of these behaviours. I know I certainly could, and I remember many of them appearing in school reports and discussions at my school parents' evenings.

The behaviours in this list are almost universal during adolescence, and while your young person may not exhibit all of them all the time, it's highly likely that you'll have come across all of them to some extent by the time your young person turns twenty-one.

Executive functions

Executive functions, or EFs, is an umbrella term used to describe a range of cognitive – or mental – processes that control skills relating to decision making, completing tasks and emotion regulation. EFs enable us to study, work and engage with others; they are like the internal drivers of our behaviour that control our reactions to situations. EFs start to develop in early childhood. However, they do not fully mature until adulthood, with proficiency obtained in the mid- to late twenties. EFs mostly sit in the frontal lobe, the last area of the brain to complete myelination. (Myelin is a fatty sheath which surrounds a long, cable-like section of neurons – nerve cells – known as axons, enabling electrical signals to be transmitted as quickly as possible around the brain; myelination is the process of covering these axons with myelin.) While myelination mostly takes place during the end of pregnancy and the early years of life, the process is not complete until a young person enters their twenties.[4] Incomplete myelination during adolescence therefore means we can expect the functions of the frontal lobe to be immature.

The main executive functions are:

- **Flexible thinking** – the ability to be able to adapt to different situations, revising planned actions and rethinking approaches; for instance, coming up with a new solution to a problem when the previous one didn't work out as expected.
- **Emotional control** – the ability to recognise and regulate your own feelings so that you can complete activities; for instance, recovering from disappointment at not being able to do something and remaining calm afterwards.
- **Impulse control** – the ability to think about how to behave, considering potential consequences of behaviour and preventing yourself from behaving in a socially inappropriate way; for instance, not shouting out in a classroom or workplace.
- **Self-monitoring** – the ability to evaluate your own behaviour and actions, including your own strengths and weaknesses, considering how you impact others and using this knowledge to improve yourself; for instance, calmly receiving feedback in a work meeting or from a teacher and acting on constructive criticism.
- **Planning and prioritisation of time** – the ability to organise your time, understanding the urgency of a task and the time available to you; for instance, pencilling in one hour in the evening to complete your homework or work report, before playing on your phone.
- **Organising** – the ability to keep track of important

information, utilising a helpful structure; for instance, keeping a list of groceries that have run out to take shopping with you.

- **Working memory** – the ability to utilise stored information in your mind to help you to complete an activity; for instance, using a mind map or mnemonic to help you revise for a test or an exam.
- **Task initiation** – the ability to get started on a task without procrastinating or becoming overwhelmed, combined with the ability to work hard until the task is completed; for instance, getting started on housework, without delay, and continuing until the room is tidy and clean.

Having read through this list, score yourself as follows:

- 'Always achieves' this executive function = 2 points
- 'Sometimes achieves' this executive function = 1 point
- 'Never achieves' this executive function = 0 points

Most adults who are neurotypical (more on this later in this chapter) would score somewhere between eight and sixteen points. Most young people, however, would score significantly lower because of their brain development. Yet the sad reality is that if you were to eavesdrop on any conversation about young people, I can almost guarantee that you would hear an adult complaining about their EF abilities, whether that's procrastination, emotional outbursts, inflexibility, stubborn behaviour, a lack of introspection or total disorganisation.

Undoubtedly, it is exhausting raising young people who have immature EF skills, but can you imagine how difficult it is to *be* the young person? Of course, you don't have to imagine too hard because you've already been there. Maybe you were frequently shouted at for never tidying your room? Maybe you got into trouble for always forgetting to do your chores or hand in your homework on time? Perhaps you remember getting angry and saying things you didn't mean in the heat of the moment? Perhaps you remember the adults in your life telling you that you needed to change and 'grow up'? Maybe you internalised these attacks on your character and grew to believe that you *were* 'lazy' or 'useless', or maybe, like me, that you were 'stroppy'. The thing is, you never were. You were simply being a young person, with a young person's brain, just like the young person in your life today. It wasn't your fault. And it isn't theirs. It's neuroscience.

EXECUTIVE FUNCTIONS: FIRST FIX VERSUS SECOND FIX

If you've ever had building work completed on your home, bought a new property, or you work in the construction industry, you'll be familiar with the terms 'first fix' and 'second fix'. Both phases happen after the shell of the property, or extension, is completed, when the walls and roof are in place. During the first fix, essential electrical, plumbing and carpentry work is carried out – cables needed for light fittings, plug sockets and appliances are installed, pipework is run for heating and water, and stairs, floors, windows and external doors will be fitted. The second fix involves more fine tuning and finishing. Internal doors are fitted alongside skirting boards and architrave, plug sockets are wired in and mounted on the walls, light fixtures are fitted, bathroom suites are plumbed in and walls plastered, ready for decorating.

If we compare adults and young people to first and second fixes, adults are a finished second fix, while young people are still very much in the first-fix stage. Young people have all the wiring in place for executive functions – the wires are in the metaphorical 'wall' of the brain, ready and waiting, but the electrician has yet to come along and connect them, so that when they plug something in, the circuitry works. Time and experiences act as the electrician for our young people. With repeated experiences and interactions with others, a young person's brain connectivity increases as the neural pathways are reinforced. Any excess neural connections that are not reinforced with repeated experiences will be pruned out, leaving only the strongest, fastest ones. The brain functions on a 'use-it-or-lose-it' basis, so encouraging young people to embrace different experiences, utilising as many EFs as possible, will allow their brains to wire up in the most helpful way.

Similarly, unhelpful behaviour that young people use a lot is reinforced via strengthened neural networks. This means that if they are treated harshly by the adults in their lives, and are used to being fearful and anxious, then these feelings will be reinforced as they grow into adults and, ultimately, they will learn to handle conflict with others in this way, too. If we want young people to grow to be calm and regulated, with good EF capabilities, we – as adults – need to resolve issues with them in a calm and mature way. We can view ourselves as the carpenters, electricians and plumbers of the second fix because our own actions and reactions shape the second fix of our young people's brains.

All young people make mistakes; they all fail to control impulses and emotions, fail to prioritise and organise their time, fail to see their impact on others, fail to be flexible and fail to reflect on their actions – not because they are 'naughty' or being deliberately rude, but because their brains are still developing the connections for higher cognitive functions.

How we react, guide and support them during these years provides some of the most precious neurological shaping opportunities.

How thinking changes in adolescence

As well as the development of EFs, the way the brain processes thoughts also changes during adolescence, specifically thinking processes that use abstraction and reason.

Abstract thinking refers to an individual's ability to understand concepts that are not immediately tangible or observable. For instance, ideas that use metaphors, emotions, or notions such as freedom or faith. Abstract thinking improves with age, partly because of lived experience, partly because of language development and partly because of brain development. Abstract thinking seems to have a link with a specific area of the prefrontal cortex, the last area of the brain to mature, and the area responsible for EFs.[5] Young people may therefore struggle to understand and engage with concepts that involve abstract-thinking skills, which, in turn, can lead to difficulties with talking about emotions, analysing problems and putting things into perspective.

Rational thinking – the ability to use logic and reason to understand the world, without an overly emotional viewpoint – is, once again, the domain of the prefrontal cortex, and is a skill not fully developed until the mid- to late twenties. As a result, young people can often struggle with making rational, well thought-through decisions and may, instead, tend towards poor judgement and hastily made decisions. Adults tend to make decisions engaging their prefrontal cortex, which involves weighing up pros and cons and thinking about any future consequences, whereas young people tend to process information using the amygdala (the seat of emotions in the brain) more. This, unsurprisingly, makes young people far more emotional and far less rational than adults, focusing much more on the here and now than considering future repercussions of their choices.

A young person's brain is still developing connections between the rational and decision-making parts, which explains so many of the issues parents and carers face. So much of young people's behaviour is irrational. When they make mistakes, or 'misbehave', they often cannot explain why they behaved in that way. I remember vividly when one of my teens (then around fifteen) was in trouble at school for scratching a fork up and down the metal legs of a table during a lesson. I was called into school for a meeting with my son and his head teacher. The teacher described what had happened, told me how inappropriate it was and informed me that my son would receive an after-school detention as a sanction. At no point did he consider the cause of the behaviour, and so when he asked if I had any questions, I said I had two. The first was to my son: 'Why did you do that?' My son replied, 'I don't know. It made a funny noise; it's like my brain wasn't working properly and I didn't even think about whether I should do it or not. I'm sorry.' The second was to the teacher: 'How will a detention help here?' To me, this behaviour was classic for a fifteen-year-old, lacking abstract and rational thought processes, with immature executive functions. Spending time in detention, I argued, would not change his brain development. In the meeting my son had already apologised and promised he would (try to) not do anything like this again. He had already faced the embarrassment of being removed from the classroom, as well as me being called into a meeting. We had also discussed that if he found cutlery in the classroom again he should give it to the teacher. So what purpose would a punishment (detention) serve here? The teacher could not answer me, aside from telling me that the school had a 'zero-tolerance' behaviour policy. I left the meeting feeling that my son was not the only one demonstrating a lack of abstract and rational thought that day.

Response to stress

Can you remember the last time your young person lost something important and was running late to get to school, college or work? They were probably rushing around your home frantically, yelling at you to help, getting progressively more angry or dissolving into tears. Sound familiar? Young people tend to be overly emotional, reactive and fearful during times of stress or pressure because the amygdala is well developed, but they don't yet have mature EFs or rational-thinking skills, enabling them to organise their thoughts, problem solve or control their impulses. In the same situation, adults are likely to be far calmer and more collected, engaging rational thinking, working memory and emotion-control skills to be able to think back to the last time they saw the item and using abstract-thinking skills to mentally walk back to the last place they had it. Expecting young people to act like us in times of stress is futile. What our young people need in such situations is an adult sharing their calm, not adding to the chaos with their own dysregulated behaviour by shouting or punishing them.

Response to reward

Have you ever wondered why young people are so keen on receiving social media likes? Or why they spend hours trying to win a computer game? Things that seem inconsequential to us as adults, can be entirely different to young people because of the rewards they bring.

Young people are naturally dopamine seeking. Dopamine is

a chemical secreted by the brain leading to feelings of pleasure (many call it the 'feelgood hormone'). An area in the centre of the brain known as the ventral striatum is activated when we do (or think about doing) something that brings us pleasure or reward, and it is linked to moods, motivation and addiction. Research has found that during adolescence, the ventral striatum is more closely linked to rewards and appears to be more reactive than it is during both earlier childhood and adulthood.[6] Adults are more likely to override the drive to seek pleasure impulsively by engaging the sensible prefrontal cortex, whereas young people are more likely to give in to the lure of pleasure and reward more easily. An hour doing chores or homework is no match for the dopamine high of one last go on *Fortnite* or another hour on TikTok.

Risk taking

Risk taking goes hand in hand with reward seeking and is one area of young people's behaviour that is directly impacted by hormones. As we discussed earlier in this chapter, increased levels of testosterone seem to increase risk-taking behaviour in both boys and girls. When we add immature EFs to the equation, alongside still-developing abstract- and rational-thinking skills, we have the perfect melting pot for risky behaviour.

If you've ever driven around your town, city or village at the end of the school day, you'll probably have noticed hordes of secondary-school children walking in the road, completely oblivious to any vehicles. Sometimes they push each other into oncoming traffic 'for a laugh', sometimes they dart out in front of you to collect a dropped or thrown ball. In this respect, junior-school children can seemingly be more mature than those in high school.

Risk taking in adolescence also appears to increase when

young people are with their peers. Research studying risk taking while young people were operating a driving simulator found that they 'drove' better when 'travelling' without a passenger.[7] The study required participants to stop when they saw a red light and found that young people were very likely to stop when in the simulator alone. When they were 'driving' with a peer, however, they were significantly less likely to stop when they observed a red light. If we relate this to the previous point of young people being reward seeking, it seems that they take more risks when with others because they receive social rewards from the connection with them, which make them feel good. This study raises real-life concerns for parents and carers of young people to be aware of when their young person learns to drive.

Empathy

'Why can't you think about others more? You're so selfish!'

This is a phrase uttered by many parents and carers of young people. And the thing is, it's true. Young people *are* less empathetic than adults, and for good reason, too. You see, young people need to focus on themselves during adolescence – they need to work out who they are, what they believe in, who they want to be friends with, what career they would like to go into and more. They have to spend a lot of time thinking about themselves because they have so many decisions to make. Throw immature EFs into the mix and our young people need plenty of time to allow them to complete the introspection necessary for this stage of life. They simply cannot spend the time focusing on others that they need to spend looking inwards.

This doesn't mean, however, that they don't care about others, nor does it mean that they do not grasp the concept of empathy. They do both of these and are certainly not the callous, selfish, uncaring people that they are often made out to be in the media or in online discussions. During adolescence, young people develop a more nuanced Theory of Mind (or ToM). ToM is the capacity to understand the individual views, beliefs and feelings of others, and the knowledge that these differ from our own. While ToM mostly develops in earlier childhood, research has shown that it continues to mature into early adulthood.[8]

How can you make your young person more empathetic? This is a question that I'm asked a lot, and the answer is simple: you show more empathy towards them. Treating young people with empathy, kindness and respect is the most powerful route to teaching them to behave this way themselves. You cannot, however, override biology, so if you find yourself doubting whether your efforts are working, trust that they are, but view them more as planting and nurturing a seed with patience, rather than constantly looking for a sprouting seedling as proof. The growth will come; you just have to be patient. We'll talk more about showing empathy for our young people in Chapter 4, when we discuss something called 'mind-minded' parenting.

Attention spans

Many media sources call young people today 'the TikTok generation' and blame the social media app for destroying their attention spans. We'll talk more about how screen time affects young people in Chapter 7, but for now I'd like you to consider the differences between correlation and causation.

Causation means that something has directly caused something else to happen, in this case the suggestion that TikTok has caused young people today to have poor attention. Correlation, on the other hand, considers the relationship between two things, without implying that one causes the other. They may simply coexist alongside each other. In this case, is something else causing the lowered attention spans that we observe when young people are drawn to social media and perhaps mistakenly imply that the social media is the cause, rather than a correlated variable? Is there another cause at play? Would young people still have short attention spans even if the internet didn't exist? Quite likely.

I think this is another case of us misremembering our youth. We didn't have mobile phones to entertain us, but we would often daydream during classes. I remember playing with a friend's hair during a boring assembly at school and picking at blades of grass during dull events outside. We may not have had smartphones, but we weren't the experts in attention that we perhaps think we were. Arguably, attention requires EF skills, and we know that these are still developing in young people, so it is understandable that they may struggle with attention more than adults. Having said that, there is research showing that attention spans are decreasing in modern times, but this is across the board, not just in adolescence, so unless younger children and elderly people are also addicted to TikTok, it's likely the cause is something else entirely.[9]

Is the teen brain inferior to that of an adult?

In short, no. In fact, in many ways it's significantly more impressive. The information we've discussed in this chapter may seem to refer to a young person's brain as somehow incomplete, or inadequate, but teen brains are actually amazing. The amount of change that is happening, with new connections, myelination, pruning and processing of new experiences is astonishing. Rather than being a sort of 'poor relation' of the adult brain, the teen brain is arguably superior – it just makes young people act in ways that adults struggle with.

Differently wired brains

While brain development and behaviour are different for every single young person, the research we have discussed so far in this chapter has focused on those who are neurotypical, not displaying any atypical neurological behaviours. In the UK, research has found that just under 3 per cent of adolescents have a diagnosis of autism, while between 2 and 7 per cent of adolescents are believed to have attention deficit hyperactivity disorder (ADHD), with another 5 per cent thought to struggle with symptoms, but sitting just under the criteria for diagnosis.[10,11] Many young people remain undiagnosed completely or receive late diagnoses, with 28 per cent not receiving a diagnosis of autism until they are at secondary school.[12] My own son was not diagnosed with ADHD until he was fifteen, despite the fact that I knew he was affected from the age of five. And many parents and young people battle to be taken seriously in a system that is underfunded and overwhelmed, while a lot of them fall through the cracks.

Life is hard enough for a young person, but if they are non-neurotypical, whether diagnosed or otherwise, things can be much harder. Frustratingly, autism and ADHD are commonly misunderstood, and stereotypes abound. And because of these stereotypes many people miss out on a diagnosis and the support that should (but sadly doesn't always) come with it. Girls in particular are overlooked, as symptoms of both autism and ADHD may look very different to those most people expect and associate with boys. Girls are therefore significantly less likely to be diagnosed with both autism and ADHD than boys. Young people, especially girls, can also be adept at 'masking' – trying to fit in by mirroring the behaviour of neurotypical young people, which is, understandably, exhausting.

What are some of the signs of autism in girls?

- Perfectionism
- Shyness
- Social withdrawal
- Friendship difficulties
- Anxiety
- People-pleasing behaviour
- Being very quiet
- Having intense special interests
- Difficulty managing emotions

Signs of ADHD in girls can mirror those of autism, but it is important to understand that attention deficit can exist without hyperactivity, in which case it is known as ADD. Instead of the 'boisterous', loud and constantly moving around stereotype that many people think of when discussing ADHD, girls may be quiet, forgetful and disorganised daydreamers.

My parenting advice doesn't change if a young person is not neurotypical because I focus on treating each young person as an individual. Most of the behaviours that we struggle with in our young people are heightened when their brains are differently wired and it is important to reset expectations of them accordingly at home and at school, and at university or work. Regrettably, our world, and especially our education system, is not set up to support young people who are not neurotypical. Knowledge in education and workplaces is still embarrassingly scant, and support, even though it may be promised, is often inadequate or non-existent. Once again, it is left to parents and carers to stand up for their young people.

Your young person cannot help the way their brain is wired, and all too often the behaviours that are symptoms of their condition, as opposed to naughtiness or deliberate defiance, end up being punished. This constant punishment can dent self-esteem that may already be low.

If young people are not diagnosed, especially girls and those young people who mask, this inauthentic living can cause huge negative consequences to their mental health. If your young person is – or you suspect that they are – non-neurotypical, then being their advocate and providing unwavering support is key.

WHY ARE INCIDENCES OF AUTISM AND ADHD INCREASING?

It is true that diagnoses of autism rose by almost 800 per cent in the UK in the twenty years between 1998 and 2018.[13] ADHD diagnosis rates are also rising. Does this mean that we are over-diagnosing children? Or that something in modern life is causing this supposed epidemic?

In reality, it is most likely that increasing diagnoses are due to simply that – the ability of modern medicine and scientific understanding to recognise young people who deviate from so-called 'normal' neurological development. Young people have always had autism and ADHD, but were just dismissed as the 'naughty' ones. Some people may claim that 'labelling' young people serves no purpose; others criticise a diagnosis as 'trendy'. But what these people are really showing is a lack of awareness and understanding. Receiving a diagnosis and, in the case of ADHD, potentially taking medication to help take the edge off the symptoms, can be life changing. In my son's case, medication (a choice that was made by him) was incredibly helpful. Within the first week he said to me, 'It's like my brain has calmed down. I can think clearly now!' Others may decide they would rather be medication free, but the important thing here is choice, and respect for your young person's decision. If a diagnosis can help others, but especially your young person, to understand their behaviour and may also bring more support, why would that ever be a bad thing?

In a world that tries so hard to change how young people behave, one of the most powerful things a parent or carer can do is to accept them as they are. Young people cannot change how their brains work today; they cannot magically develop mature, adult-level thinking skills, no matter how much we attempt to reward or punish them or subject them to lectures and consequences. If, instead of focusing our efforts on trying to change them, we worked *with* them and helped them to understand their marvellous brains, I believe everything would be very different, especially for those young people who are neurodiverse.

So much of what we describe as 'attitude', 'rudeness', 'disrespect' and 'laziness' is normal for young people. Many of their most frustrating behaviours don't need to be disciplined out of them. Instead, they need our support, guidance and patience. Yes, this is hard for us, but in the end, understanding and nurturance are key to caring for our young people, both now and in the future.

The best way we can help our young people's brains to finish developing traits relating to confidence, calmness, empathy and consideration for others, is to embody these traits ourselves in our day-to-day dealings with them. It's time to accept our young people for who they are, and this brings us neatly to the next chapter, which is all about the young person's sense of belonging in the world.

Chapter 3

Belonging and Developing Identities

*To be yourself in a world that is constantly trying to
make you something else is the greatest accomplishment.*
RALPH WALDO EMERSON, American philosopher and essayist

'All you need is love.'

Almost sixty years ago, The Beatles neatly summarised some of the most complex and impactful psychological research, not only of the time, but of the future, too. Everybody, no matter their age, needs to feel a sense of belonging and unconditional love, that they are understood and can be their authentic selves, in order to be happy. For young people, this need is heightened and, as their identity develops, they innately search for connection, recognition and belonging among their peers, colleagues, romantic, platonic and familial relationships.

If you've read any of my other books, you've probably heard me talk about Abraham Maslow and his 'hierarchy of needs' before. If you haven't and you're new to the concept, or you'd like a quick refresher, this next section is for you. If you're well versed in Maslow already, feel free to skip it.

Maslow's hierarchy of needs

In 1943, psychologist Abraham Maslow published his 'Theory of Human Motivation'.[1] Part of his theory included his idea of a hierarchy of needs which separates the physical and emotional needs of people into five separate stages, each of which builds upon the last, like a stepladder. Maslow placed the most basic needs for survival first, providing a solid physical foundation for more emotional steps to follow. The pinnacle, which Maslow named 'self-actualisation', can be achieved only if an individual fulfils the needs in the previous lower stages. Maslow believed that self-actualisation – the psychological state of being fulfilled, achieving everything a person sets out to achieve in life, and being genuinely happy and in control of their emotions – was the pinnacle of human development, but it could only be reached if the individual felt safe, was nurtured emotionally and physically, felt supported and unconditionally loved, with a sense of belonging, in childhood and in the present day.

The illustration on p. 48 shows the stages of Maslow's hierarchy of needs.

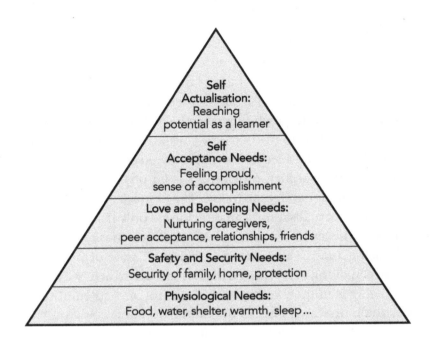

The adolescent need for belonging

Without a feeling of belonging, as described on the previous page, we can struggle with low self-esteem and confidence and question our purpose in life.

For young people, belonging usually has three main sources: their families, their school, university or workplace, and their friends or romantic relationships. A lack of a sense of belonging has been linked with negative consequences in both physical and mental health.[2] While belonging is undoubtedly important at all ages, it is paramount during adolescence and closely linked to the development of self-esteem (the level of Maslow's stages that sits above belonging).[3]

An established sense of belonging at school during the teen years is a reliable predictor of not only attitudes to learning and academic achievement, but also a reduction of challenging be-haviours at school, mental-health issues, and even risk-taking behaviour, smoking and unsafe sexual practices.[4] Fostering their young person's sense of belonging at home, therefore, should be a major goal for parents and carers, because the more they feel safe, secure, accepted and loved unconditionally at home, the more likely they are to be happy, confident and successful in other areas of their life. Feeling that they belong and are appre-ciated in their family is a crucial foundation for them to climb Maslow's pyramid.

Social media also plays a role in a young person's feeling of belonging, with research finding that adolescents who reported feeling a high sense of belonging when using social media showed fewer mental-health issues.[5] While an overreliance on social media and overuse can be detrimental to young people (an issue we will discuss in Chapter 7), parents and carers should also understand that there is a positive side. Our social networks when we were in our teens may have consisted of long telephone calls on wired phones, writing to pen pals and calling in person at a friend's house to invite them to hang out with us, but our young people today connect online. We'll talk much more about the use of the internet later in this book, because we cannot ignore the importance of the connections that it brings.

The need for acceptance

Do you remember your parents, carers or teachers comparing you to a sibling or a peer when you were a teen? 'Why can't you do better at school like your sister?' 'Your brother is so much easier and better behaved than you – why can't you be more like him?' 'If you tried as hard as others in your class, you would do much better.'

These sorts of statements, as I suspect you well know from

experience, do nothing to help young people change their behaviour for the better and they don't motivate them to improve their thinking either. What they do is eat away at their confidence and self-esteem, little by little.

When I was a teen, I was often compared to the daughter of a family friend who was one year older than me. She was a natural academic, smart, beautiful, emotionally mature and always kind and respectful. I, on the other hand, was a typical young person, my efforts at school were sporadic and my emotions often got the better of me. I began to really resent this girl every time I was compared to her and, perhaps more importantly, I also began to resent my parents. At no point did their comparisons make me feel inspired to improve anything about myself. In fact, I began to question my parents' love for me and clearly remember one day, saying to my mother, 'If you think she's so wonderful, then perhaps you should try to adopt her and I'll leave home'.

I'm an only child, so never had comparisons to any siblings, but I was compared to my cousins regularly. Now, as a mother of four young people, I try to not compare my children to each other. Each of them is wonderfully unique, with their own strengths and weaknesses, and comparison would not only be pointless, but damaging, too. Does this mean I stick perfectly to this rule? Sadly not, and there are times, when one of them has been particularly trying, and a comparison has slipped out of my mouth, but it's something that I work hard at, and is still a work in progress. Measuring against others, whether related or not, is problematic and harmful, yet it is something most young people face, whether at home or at school, college, university or even in the workplace.

What young people really need is unconditional acceptance of the person that they are, not who they could be or who you want them to be. We are all human *beings*, not human *becomings*, and yet so many young people are raised with a constant view on who they will be 'as an adult'. When parents and carers focus so heavily on the future, they forget that a young person is somebody today and it is their present self that needs our support, acceptance and unconditional regard. The more young people feel accepted for who they are in this moment in time, the more likely they are to develop positive self-esteem and confidence levels which, in turn, help them to fulfil their potential as they grow.

Research has shown that parental acceptance of young people is linked to their mental health, with a direct correlation between higher parental acceptance and better mental health versus a lack of parental acceptance and poorer mental health.[6] The impact of parental acceptance isn't just limited to observable effects during adolescence – it can last into adulthood, too, with further research showing that during the teenage years it can be linked to levels of further-educational attainment in early adulthood.[7] This research is a great example of why parents and carers should rein in comparison and pressure during the school years and, instead, aim simply to practise acceptance of their young person. Thinking back to Maslow's hierarchy of needs and the pinnacle of self-actualisation, we know that young people need to feel they belong in order to reach their full potential, and the most crucial part of that belonging is feeling accepted by those who love and care for them.

The developing self

As young people grow, they frequently ask themselves two questions: 'Who am I now?' and 'Who do I want to be in the future?' These questions form the basis of their developing identities.

Our identities incorporate our individual beliefs, values and goals in life. They are shaped by relationships with family, friends, peers, colleagues, life experiences, social factors, time spent in school, college and university, and the expectations placed upon us by others. As a young person grows, they become more sensitive to feedback about themselves than they were when younger, especially if this is at odds with the identity that they are developing for themselves, which can be the source of many fraught disagreements and frustrations between them and their parents and carers. As a parent, you want to encourage your young person to spread their wings and become their own person, but you also want to make sure that they are safe and making the most of the opportunities offered to them. Both young people and parents naturally struggle with this dichotomy.

The development of identity spans a lifetime, and we are all always changing and shifting in our self-thoughts and beliefs, but adolescence is a unique and special time in this respect. Young people often veer between wanting to hold on to their childhoods and the past, and wanting to grow up and become independent, with a focus on their future adult selves. Often, this self-development means pushing back against parents and carers and working to establish their own identities outside of immediate family. These years are a process of self-discovery for our young people in which they play an active part, albeit often subconsciously, by choosing who they want to be around and who they influence and are influenced by. Before adolescence, your child's identity was shaped heavily by you and other close family members, but now it's time for your young person to find out who they are as an individual.

As young people get older and their abstract-thinking skills develop, they start to consider their place in the wider world, and how they fit into it, both now and in the future. In the earlier years you protected your child from the scary and evil parts of the world, but now their view of it becomes more realistic, with far less limited exposure and increased understanding. It's like a protective blindfold has been taken off and, understandably, the world can seem a scary and cruel place to them, after the shielded view of their childhood. This newly acquired anxiety often adds to the push-and-pull effect young people experience with their parents and carers, and can result in them becoming overly emotional.

As they grow, young people show an increased interest in society and the world around them, forming their own social and political beliefs, which may well differ from yours. Again, this is an important step in the development of their own identities, no matter how tricky or awkward discussions at home may feel. While you may prefer an easy life, without constant questioning, doubt and criticism, these things are necessary and important for your young person's self-development, and it is your job, as an adult, not to take their questioning and criticism of your beliefs personally.

Psychological theories of identity development

Perhaps the most famous psychological theory of identity development during childhood and adolescence comes from the German/American psychotherapist Erik Erikson, who advanced his theory of psychosocial development in the 1960s.[8] The main goal of adolescence, according to Erikson, is the formation of a self-identity, where young people face a turning point in their lives, trying to decide on their life choices, career, political views, beliefs and how they want to present to society. While this happens throughout the whole of an individual's life, Erikson viewed it as a linear process, with eight stages. The two stages relevant to young people are:

- Identity versus confusion (ages twelve to eighteen), where young people are experimenting with different identities and roles.

- Intimacy versus isolation (ages nineteen to twenty-nine), where young people are testing relationships involving intimacy and time spent alone.

Erikson believed that the identity crisis faced during adolescence is resolved once a young person reaches a state of identity achievement, where they feel settled and secure, and therefore any remaining identity confusion dissipates.

In the 1970s, American psychologist James Marcia built upon Erikson's work.[9] Marcia saw identity not as linear (as Erikson believed), but more about trying on different identities for a while, then moving on, back and forth, before finally deciding to commit to one. Marcia believed this identity development went through four stages, as follows:

- Identity diffusion (a state of confusion when a young person is neither exploring nor committing to an identity)
- Identity foreclosure (when a young person has committed to an identity, but without much exploration)
- Identity moratorium (when a young person is still exploring, but no commitment to an identity has yet been made)
- Identity achievement (when a young person has both explored options and made a commitment)

Marcia believed that time spent in a prolonged state of identity diffusion is linked with poorer mental health, self-esteem and confidence and more difficult friendships; he also believed that a young person can be forced into an identity-diffusion state by parents who are too controlling and prohibit exploration. If a young person is too concerned about their parents' or carers' view of them, they are essentially left in limbo identity-wise.

Similarly, if a young person feels drawn to an identity but they believe it may not be one that their parents and carers are happy with, they may associate more strongly with their peers and, ironically, the parents lose the very influence that they were so desperate to assert. This is the beginning of a young person breaking away from their parents and is an all-too-common story with those who have overly strict and controlling families. You won't change their minds, but you may just push them away.

One frequently mentioned problem with Marcia's theory is that a young person may not (and indeed often does not) fit neatly into a box; they can struggle with one part of their identity while feeling secure with another. The theory also implies that once a commitment to an identity has been made, a young person can't (or doesn't attempt to) change it, which is not true. With these criticisms in mind, a fifth state was proposed by researchers in 2012, known as 'searching moratorium'.[10] In this state, a young person re-explores and their identity still shifts in a stage that can last well into adulthood.

Adolescent egocentrism

In 1967, American psychologist David Elkind proposed his theory of adolescent egocentrism.[11] Elkind believed that during adolescence, developmental changes cause young people to become self-absorbed and to focus much more on their own perceptions of the world, to the exclusion of others. He held that young people struggle to perceive the difference between what they think others think of them and what that perception actually is. This egocentrism leads to the creation of two specific emotional states.

The first is known as an 'imaginary audience' and refers to a state where the young person believes that everybody is watching them, listening to them or judging them, almost constantly.

In this state, they may become anxious about how people will act towards them, due to the belief that they are constantly being observed. They may also think that others will judge them as negatively as they judge themselves, which naturally causes anxiety and distress in a negative-feedback loop.

Second is a state known as the 'personal fable', whereby a young person focuses on their individuality and the self-belief that nobody else is like them. Elkind held that in this state, young people think they are special and unique and that others haven't experienced the sort of thoughts they have before. This state can come across as egotistical, and disrespectful to parents and carers – however, egocentrism is a normal stage of adolescent development, as opposed to a conceited, selfish state of adulthood. The two shouldn't be confused, but they often are.

Why your young person wants to drop out of clubs and classes so often

Does your young person flit between different clubs and activities? Are you sick of them quitting only a few weeks in (especially if you've had to pay for the whole term upfront)?

When my children were younger, we went through a plethora of after-school and weekend activities, including (but not limited to – there were so many I'm sure I've forgotten several!): rugby, football, swimming, street dance, ballet, tap, modern, karate, judo, drama, piano, drumming, art club, open-mic music nights, chess and role-playing club. Most of these were abandoned within the first term, with the exception of my daughter's dance lessons, which she quit at age fifteen after thirteen years. That one especially broke my heart as dance, particularly ballet, had been a part of our lives for so long and she had achieved so many gradings, not to mention I had just bought a new pair of pointe shoes which, together with the trip to a specialist retailer in central London for a fitting, had cost close to £150. Despite my heartache, however, my daughter was done with dance and that part of her life was history, at least for the time being. Any desire to finish the last couple of grades was solely mine, and regardless of the difficulty of putting my young person's needs above my own and a subconscious desire to live out my ballet dreams vicariously through her, I knew that allowing my daughter to quit was important. She had moved on. She had tried on the dancer hat, and it didn't quite fit; she was now ready for a new hat, however much I treasured the old one.

Whatever our frustrations as parents and carers, it is important for our young people to try out different clubs, societies, activities and hobbies, to see which – if any – are a good fit. Some will be in their lives for a short time, some for longer, and others may play a central role in their identities well into adulthood. If they don't try – and, importantly, if we don't allow them to quit – they will never know which they really want to commit to. As parents and carers, we can get frustrated and angry when our young people chop and change and drop things frequently, especially when things are difficult financially, but if they feel that something doesn't suit their developing identities, they shouldn't be forced to stick with it. Ultimately, the best lesson we can take here is to check cancellation policies and ask for free trials or pay-as-you-go options for as long as possible, plus hold off buying any kit, or ask to borrow or purchase it second-hand until you are sure that the activity will 'stick'. A young person who is forced to continue an activity that they no longer enjoy because of their parents' financial investment in it is never going to fully commit to it, but they will build resentment towards their parents.

All change

It is not just a young person's activities that change. They frequently flit between different social groups and move on from beloved childhood friends to new ones (we'll talk about changing friendships more in Chapter 8). As they work to decide which groups and beliefs suit them, the best thing we can do as parents is to try not to judge or control. Over time, young people will develop new beliefs and strong commitments that may wane and change. We do them a disservice when we label this searching of self as 'just phases'. These shifting identities are still a part of them and, as we now know, incredibly important to the developing self. As parents and carers, we should really try to be open to this experimentation and support our young people. Perhaps their current choices will stick, perhaps they won't, but what really matters is that to them, acceptance is key.

I've always thought that adolescence is the worst time to expect a young person to decide on a future career. From the age of fifteen or sixteen onwards they are shepherded into a series of choices. What do you want to do when you leave school? Which A-levels? Which college course? Which apprenticeship? Which university course? But the truth is, adolescence is the worst time to make big decisions and stick to them. If we force young people to make decisions about the future before they've even decided who they are in this moment in time, we shouldn't be surprised when they don't stick with something that feels wrong to them, and we certainly shouldn't chastise them for it if they later change their minds.

GENDER IDENTITY

A 2021 population census in England and Wales found that 1 per cent of young people aged between sixteen and twenty-four identify as transgender (trans) – that is, they feel that their gender is different to the sex registered at their birth; this figure is almost double that of adults, with an incidence rate of 0.54 per cent.[12] Many young people who identify as trans, later 'desist' or feel congruence with their birth gender as time passes. Some estimate that this is the case in up to 80 per cent of young people who initially identify as trans. However, this research has been criticised for methodological reasons and it is difficult to assess the true incidence.[13]

Young people with autism are significantly more likely to report gender dysphoria (feeling discomfort and distress because there is a mismatch between their biological sex and the gender they identify with) than those who are neu-rotypical.[14] There is to date, however, no consensus on the explanation for the increased incidence of gender dysphoria among young people with autism. Some believe that there is simply a correlation between those who are trans and autism, without one causing the other, while others hold that the link has more to do with the difficulties establishing a self-identity and fitting in with societal expectations faced by young people with autism.

Whatever the reasons, young people who are struggling with their gender identity need to feel unconditionally ac-cepted by their parents and carers. They need adults to listen to them and take them seriously. Their feelings may be temporary and, in time, they may feel more at ease with a lessening (or sometimes even disappearance) of gender dysphoria. Alternatively, their feelings may intensify and may be permanent. These decisions are not ones that a parent or carer should attempt to make for their young person, and they are certainly not feelings that should be ignored, ridiculed or shamed. No young person has ever felt less trans because their parents told them it was 'just a phase', but words like this can severely damage the young-person–parent bond and the young person's trust in the adults in their life. If your young person confides in you that they feel they may be trans, then seeking help from medical professionals and support groups is the best place to start, as well as working through your own feelings and biases, so you can fully support them.

Ikigai – finding a sense of purpose

Have you heard the term Ikigai? It's a Japanese concept (based on the words 'iki', meaning 'life', and 'kai', meaning 'shell') that encompasses the meaning of life and living with purpose. The philosophy is believed to date back hundreds of years, before it was brought to wider attention by psychiatrist Mieko Kamiya, whose book *On the Meaning of Life* was published in Japanese in the 1960s.[15] The concept recently became popular in Western society after the publication of the book *Ikigai: The Japanese Secret to a Long and Happy Life* by Héctor García and Francesc Miralles in 2016.[16]

The modern interpretation of Ikigai is a meeting of four components which lead an individual to feel a sense of belonging and purpose (particularly when it comes to career choices) when they do what they love, what the world needs, what they're good at and what they can get paid for. This combination may seem out of the reach of young people, especially those still trying to decide what they want to do for a career, but it provides a good starting point for conversations and considering options and also helps them to see that they are more than 'adults in training' or 'future employees'. Placing a focus on a sense of fulfilment and purpose, rather than academics and fitting in to society, is far more helpful to a young person who is working hard to develop their identity and is something I have discussed often with my own young people. Imagine how much happier adults would be today if these ideas had been embraced in their own adolescence? Research shows that areas of the brain responsible for the thought processes involved in Ikigai develop during adolescence, with increasing connectivity in the frontal lobe of the brain.[17] When young people embrace the idea of Ikigai, it is possible not only to improve their wellbeing, but also to strengthen these neurological connections and, in the end, their sense of identity and purpose.

How to support your young person's developing identity

In this chapter, we have looked at numerous ways in which parents and carers can support their young people while they develop their sense of self and identity. Here they are in a nutshell:

- Offer unconditional acceptance of your young person as they are today, with a focus on them as a human 'being', not a human 'becoming'.
- Act as a sounding board and guide towards information, but don't take over and try to control, or even steer, your young person's path in life.
- Allow your young person to try on different metaphorical hats, without judgement or ridicule.
- Encourage exploration of different activities, hobbies

and social groups, without putting pressure on them to
commit long term.

- Don't compare your young person to others, especially
  if those others are their siblings, other family members
  or close friends.
- Don't belittle your young person's choices, activities or
  interests.
- Don't try to force your young person into activities,
  choices or beliefs of yours, or take it personally if
  they hold different beliefs to you, or dislike activities
  you love.
- Let them know it's normal to still be figuring out who
  they are; there is no rush to make any decisions or
  commit to a certain identity yet – they have the rest of
  their life for that.
- Let them know that anxiety and doubts about having
  to choose and commit to an identity are normal and
  common, and experienced by most adolescents.
- Don't just say 'be yourself'. While this may seem like
  a positive phrase, it may place more pressure on them
  if they're struggling to know who they are at the
  present time.
- Don't rush them to decide on a future path, whether
  academic or work related.
- Let them make mistakes and change their mind.
  Mistakes are an important part of developing an
  identity, because if they don't try – and sometimes fail –
  they won't know if something is right for them or not.
- Don't jump to conclusions about their behaviour or
  their choices. Parents and carers often read too much
  into these and extrapolate wildly.
- Reassure your young person that they will always
  belong in your family and that you are a safe place for
  them to express themselves.

- If your young person is struggling with their
  identity, particularly relating to their gender or
  neurodivergence, help them to access professional
  support, and never indicate that they are going
  through a temporary phase or try to force an identity
  on them.

When I was writing this chapter, I was frequently drawn to a quote that is commonly attributed to my children's favourite author, Dr. Seuss, but may also be from US presidential advisor Bernard M. Baruch: 'Be who you are and say what you feel, because those who mind don't matter and those who matter don't mind'. I can't think of any better way to sum up the information we have covered here. If we want to stay close to our young people as they grow, developing their identities and searching for belonging, we must be the people who matter to them and who don't mind, or judge, their exploration and behaviour. The more we can do this, the more we will build them up and help to protect their mental health, which is precisely the theme of the next chapter.

Chapter 4

Confidence and Emotional Wellbeing

Self-esteem is made up primarily of two things: feeling lovable and feeling capable.
JACK CANFIELD, American author

What does the word 'confidence' mean to you? Whenever I give talks to large groups of parents and carers of young people and ask them which traits and qualities they would most like their young people to possess, 'confidence' is always in the top three answers.

We talk lots about the desire for children to be confident, almost from the moment of birth. We want babies to be confident to sleep alone, we want toddlers to be confident to play alone, we want preschoolers to be confident going into nursery alone, we want school-aged children to be confident making new friends and trying new things ... Yet I don't think we spend enough time thinking about what this so-called confidence means to us and, most importantly, to our children. Do we mean that we want them to be happy away from us? To have good relationships with others? To be extroverted, or adventurous? Or something else? Perhaps 'confidence' is used as a catch-all term to encompass good mental health, which we hope will positively infiltrate all elements of an individual's life. Or perhaps it means different things to different people? The dictionary definition of confidence is: 'the quality of being certain of your abilities or of having trust in people, plans or the future'.[1] So perhaps it really boils down to trust – trusting in others to support you and act in your best interests and, above all, trusting in yourself.

Ironically, although most of us want our young people to be confident, we don't want them to be *too* confident, because we often associate perceived overconfidence with cockiness, arrogance, rudeness, stubbornness or something that many adults simply refer to as 'attitude'. And no parent wants to raise young people with those traits. No, we want just the right amount of confidence, so that our young people are still easy enough to be around, still listen to us and still show a certain amount of compliance. Basically, we want them to be easy to raise. But the question is this: is what's best for us as parents and carers really what's best for our young people? I'm not so sure.

What worries young people today?

When researching this book, I asked a hundred teenagers whether they felt it was harder or easier to be a teen today than in previous generations. A huge 91 per cent told me they felt it was harder today. Of the remainder, 6 per cent said they felt it was no different and only 3 per cent told me they thought life was easier today. Looking at the results of the poll was sobering. We hear much in the news about young people struggling with their mental health, especially since the Covid pandemic. In 2022, statistics collected by researchers leading the Mental Health of Children and Young People in England Survey showed that one in four sixteen- to twenty-four-year-olds and one in six seven- to sixteen-year-olds had a probable mental-health problem.[2] Five years previously, the statistics were very different, with one in ten young people experiencing a probable mental-health problem.

What is the cause of this decline in young people's mental health? As you would expect, there is no simple answer, but changes in the education system, which places more pressure on young people (something we will discuss in much more depth in Chapter 6), the impacts of unregulated screen time and social media (again, something we will come back to in Chapter 7), Covid lockdowns and the impact of economic pressures, combined with chronic underfunding and understaffing in adolescent mental-health services have provided the perfect storm for problems.

I asked the same hundred teens if they could share some of their worries and fears with me. This is what some of them told me:

- 'I worry about my safety when I'm out "on the streets".'
- 'I feel that there is a constant pressure to be perfect at everything.'
- 'I stress about keeping up with social expectations of me.'
- 'I constantly feel the need to fit in with my friends and classmates.'
- 'I struggle with dealing with social media.'
- 'My biggest worry is difficult friendships and how to manage them.'
- 'I worry about not being able to get a job to support myself when I'm older.'
- 'I'm worried about all the war constantly happening in the world.'
- 'Climate change makes me really fearful for my future and our world.'

- 'I'm really worried that I won't do as well as everyone hopes I will in my GCSEs.'
- 'I'm nervous to start university and worried that I won't get the grades I need to get in.'
- 'There is so much hatred in the world, and I'm scared about how much worse it will get.'
- 'My main anxiety is about the environment and the government is not doing anything about it.'
- 'My mental health isn't very good, and I don't seem to be able to improve it.'
- 'I'm worried about the cost of living. My parents are struggling, and I can't see how I'll ever be able to afford to live alone.'
- 'Every day there is a new war or conflict. It just feels like the world isn't a very nice place.'

Fifty-five per cent of the teens polled told me that they were unhappy at school or college, currently. When asked to extrapolate, most spoke often about the academic pressure, exams, being given too much homework and not being able to study subjects that they enjoy.

Too often, adults dismiss the thoughts of young people as naïve, inconsequential and shallow. They talk about living in 'the real world' and how teens today are mollycoddled, wrapped in cotton wool and act like snowflakes. But in reality, young people often worry about similar things to adults. They are concerned about the state of the world, the economy, the wellbeing of their friends and families, and their current studies and future careers. These are all real and valid concerns and should be treated as such by adults.

Locus of control

The concept of locus of control (LoC) is used to describe the thought processes individuals have concerning how much control they have over events that happen in their own lives. The idea was first coined by psychologist Julian Rotter in the 1950s. If an individual believes that they have 'free will' and full control over the events that happen in their own lives, they are considered to have an internal LoC. If, on the other hand, they believe that the events that happen in their life are due to fate, luck or other supernatural forces and that they have little personal control, they are said to have an external LoC. Rotter believed that people would sit somewhere on a sliding scale between the two extremes of internal and external.

In adolescence, a young people's LoC may look something like the following:

- **External**: 'There's no point revising for exams; it's all down to luck and how easy or hard the paper is on the day.' 'There's no point me making decisions about my future; whatever will be will be.' 'I'll just let fate decide for me; I can't really control anything.'
- **Internal**: 'If I revise and work hard, I can do well in my exams.' 'I can plan for my future career and follow the steps necessary to achieve my goals.' 'I am in charge of my own life and destiny.'

A young person with an external LoC takes a passive approach to life, feeling that they have little control over anything, whereas a young person with an internal LoC takes an active, motivated approach to achieving their goals. Those with a more external LoC are invariably more prone to poorer mental health, and research has shown that young people with an internal LoC are more resilient, particularly during times of intense stress.[3,4,5]

How can you foster a more internal LoC in young people?

It may sound obvious, but talking with your young person about LoC and helping them to understand their predominant thought patterns can make a real difference. It is so rare that adults spend time with young people explaining how our thinking works and how we can change it, most likely because we were never taught this by adults when we ourselves were younger. So these sort of conversations are rare, despite their power.

Try to encourage your young person to consider their thought patterns and to question their instinctive responses to questions from others. Ideally, they would also investigate their self-talk and consider whether it tends towards being based more on an internal or external LoC. Choosing a time when this conversation flows organically is best, especially if the trigger for the conversation is the young person veering towards an external LoC. For instance, if they have an upcoming job interview, ask them how they are feeling about it and what preparation they are doing. If they tell you, 'It's pointless; I'm going to do badly anyway', or, 'I'm hoping that it will be easy and nobody else applies', that's a great opportunity to talk about external LoC and how this sort of thinking actually takes away their power.

It's important also to emphasise that trying to nurture an internal LoC isn't about trying to always ace everything, and it's OK to fail and make mistakes. The key is to use mistakes as learning opportunities to understand what they can take from the situation and work on, in order to do better in the future. In this case, that would centre on how they can work on answers to common interview questions, so that they are better prepared for future ones.

Here is a lovely acronym to share with your young person, spelling out the word 'FAIL'. The FAIL acronym can help your young person to understand that failing at something initially is not the end of the world, but instead an opportunity to learn from what went well and what didn't, in order to improve next time.

First
Attempt
In
Learning

Thinking of this acronym can help young people to shift into a more internal LoC, especially at times when they are finding things tough and life isn't going the way they'd hoped.

Talk of LoC can be used to help inspire your young person to move from a passive approach, where life just happens to them, to a more active approach – one where they feel empowered and, ultimately, more confident in themselves.

When life *is* out of control for young people

As much as we would like our young people to always feel as if they are masters of their own destinies, fully on top of everything that life throws at them, there are some things they can't control – for example, worries about war and climate change that many young people told me about in my survey (see p. 65). Concerns about the cost of living can also leave young people feeling out of control, steering them towards a more external LoC. The previously mentioned Mental Health of

Children and Young People in England Survey found that one in five teens under the age of sixteen lived in a household that had experienced a reduction in household income in the past year. Similarly, statistics show that 29 per cent of UK teens are living in poverty today.[6]

So how do you help your young person to feel they have more control in a world that feels increasingly out of control? Once again, the answer lies in communicating with them. Be open and honest. Don't try to shield them from the stark realities of the world – because however much you do so, they will discover the truth, whether through hushed conversations, snippets on TV shows, letters accidentally left on the kitchen worktop or friends talking to them at school or work. It's always better to have full control of the narrative yourself, to think carefully about how to speak to them and share information in a way that is most manageable for them. Once young people fully understand a situation, it takes some of the fear away.

Coming up with some steps they can take to try actively to help a situation is effective, too. If they're worried about the environment, perhaps they could produce a plan for your family to reduce its carbon footprint, launch a recycling plan for your local village or town, or organise a local litter-picking activity. If their concerns are about war, perhaps they could organise a collection to donate to an aid charity or write a letter to your MP, urging politicians to vote for peace. If the cost of living is the cause of worry, perhaps they could come up with some inventive ways to save money, such as collecting coupons and discount codes, using cashback websites, or find some ways to bring in a little extra cash for the family, like selling at a car boot sale or via an online marketplace. Once young people feel that they can do something to change a situation, no matter how small that something is, it helps them to feel a little more in control, which can, in turn, help to improve their mental health, as well as helping others.

Emodiversity

Raising young people in a home that fosters the importance of embracing all emotions – a concept known as emodiversity – has a protective effect on mental health and can help them to feel more confident. Research has found that those who experience more emotions are significantly healthier, not just mentally but physically, too, while a study looking specifically at adolescents found that emodiversity is protective against developing an eating disorder.[7,8]

Emodiversity involves the capacity to feel different emotions and an acceptance of them. No emotion is viewed as 'bad' or 'wrong', and an individual is not judged or labelled for feeling a certain way. Instead, all emotions are considered important, and experiencing the full spectrum of them is valued. In a world where there seems to be constant pressure on all of us to 'be happy', the idea of emodiversity is a welcome one. In short, it means it's OK to be sad, angry, frustrated or jealous, as well as happy. And considering that young people's brain development leads them to feel emotions more strongly than adults, with less ability to regulate them, understanding that having *all* the big feelings is a positive thing is a great confidence boost.

Whenever I explain the concept of emodiversity to parents and carers, I always talk about the Disney Pixar movie *Inside Out*. It is a perfect example of valuing all feelings and their expression, and is a brilliant way to understand young people. If you haven't watched it, I strongly recommend that you do. It may be billed as a children's film, but I feel it provides more valuable parenting advice than a lot of courses!

How can you increase emodiversity in your home?

The easiest starting point is simply to accept all emotions. Lose any preconceived ideas you may have that certain feelings are negative, disrespectful, unbecoming or undesirable. Let your young person know that they are safe to express all their emotions with you, and don't take them personally. Of course, to do this you also need to become more comfortable with your own emotions – both experiencing them and expressing them around your loved ones. This can be tricky for many of us who were brought up in households where emodiversity was shunned in favour of quiet obedience. Try to see embracing emodiversity as a challenge for the whole family, not just your young person, and something that can really improve the mental health of all family members, including you.

To be more accepting of all emotions, we also need to suppress our instincts to quieten them in a misguided attempt at discipline. We are too quick to jump in and correct behaviour, especially if we perceive it as disrespectful. Instead, we would be better placed to focus on the emotions behind the behaviour and let the words that accompany it slide – to see the feelings, not the jumble of impulsive language surrounding them. The next time your young person swears at you, tells you that they hate you or similar, try to suppress your instinct to yell, 'Don't you speak to me like that! Who do you think you're talking to?' and instead say, 'It sounds like you're really struggling at the moment. What can I do to help?' This doesn't make you permissive, especially not when your response is followed up with a conversation about using respectful, non-violent language in the future; you can still use discipline (more on this in the next chapter), you just make the focus deeper.

There is always a reason why young people are rude, and we

can either spend our time superficially battling the words they use and their tone of voice, or we can look for the underlying emotions and support them. Only one of these approaches works to increase confidence and self-esteem in young people. I'll let you guess which one it is!

Mind-minded parenting

Embracing emodiversity fully involves a good degree of empathy and understanding. Parents and carers of young people need to really consider how their young person feels if they are going to support all their emotions.

When we try to put ourselves in our young person's shoes and think about how they feel and what they are experiencing, particularly in times of stress and conflict, we are automatically gentler to them. It is hard to be angry and harsh towards a young person who you know is really struggling, despite the difficult outward manifestation of their feelings.

The idea of really reflecting on your young person's point of view in your interactions with them is known as 'mind-minded parenting'. Mind-mindedness is the process of understanding that others, particularly children and young people, have individual minds, with their own beliefs, thoughts and feelings. The consideration of these as a parent means that we are more likely to embrace emodiversity, and our young people can behave more authentically around us, asking us for our help when they need it.

Far too many teenagers (and yes, I do mean teens here, not young people) are too scared to talk to their parents about their real feelings, for fear of punishment, and so, in time, they stop communicating, which leads to them internalising their emotions, repressing them and pushing them inwards. We can only hold on to emotions for a certain length of time before they either start to eat away at us or explode out as violence, whether verbal or physical, towards others. Research has shown that mothers who employ mind-mindedness are more likely to raise adolescents who behave 'well' and don't exhibit antisocial behaviour with others.[9] Being mind-minded is an important way to keep channels of communication open with our young people, not just now, but in the future, too.

How to encourage your young person to open up to you more

When your son or daughter was little, I'm pretty sure you would have given anything for some peace and quiet. The never-ending questions, telling you intricate stories about something they had seen on TV or read in a book and the constant talking over you when you were trying to have a conversation with another adult were all draining. I remember sometimes locking myself in the toilet, so that I couldn't be followed, just so I could have a couple of minutes to myself. Be careful what you wish for, though, because all too soon those children grow up into young people and sometimes it feels like it's easier to get blood out of a stone than it is to get them to open up and talk to you. If this is the case for you, give these tips a try:

- When they do tell you something, make sure you listen. Put your phone down, shut your laptop, turn down the TV or close your book and really listen. Young people need to know that you value what they have to say.
- Make time for them, especially when it's inconvenient. There's only so many times a young person will hear 'in a minute, I'm busy' before they decide it's not worth trying to speak to you. Reconsider your

priorities. Is it really necessary that you carry on with what you're doing, or can you put it on hold for ten minutes while you chat with your young person?

- Embrace the late-night chats. I'm not sure what it is that makes young people love talking about big issues at midnight, but it seems universal. If you ask your young person if they're OK at 6 p.m. they're very likely to say 'yes'; fast forward six hours when you're in bed and dozing off and they'll come in and start talking, and it turns out they're not OK. These late-night chats are golden – don't waste them. However tired you are, you should always sit up and say, 'OK, let's talk!'

- Don't tease them. As tempting as it may be to re-enact the teasing you probably received from your own parents or grandparents, teasing them, especially over their romantic feelings, is a sure-fire way to guarantee they don't tell you things in the future.

- Don't dismiss their worries. Saying 'you'll be OK' is a great way to make sure that, in fact, they won't be OK. It makes them feel silly for even asking for help, undermines their confidence, and in time, they'll learn to just stop asking for help.

- Too often, we jump straight into 'advice mode', giving different options and opinions and telling our young people what we would do in their situation. Often, though, they don't want advice – they just want to offload, and if they try to do so and you pile on the advice, you just fill them up to the brim with stress again. The next time your young person asks if they can speak to you, start by saying, 'Sure. Would you like my advice or would you prefer I just listened?'

- Ease up on the punishment. If you want your young person to feel comfortable opening up to you, then you have to make them believe that they can tell you anything without fear of reprimand. I've always been clear with my young people that the worst thing they can do is lie to me, and that means I have to take a deep breath when they tell me things I don't really want to hear – because honesty is so important.

We can't force our young people to talk to us, and indeed we shouldn't, but the way we ourselves behave and our approach to emodiversity and mind-mindedness lets our young people know that we are safe people to speak to. And when they feel safe, they are far more likely to open up.

WHAT TO DO IF YOU'RE WORRIED ABOUT YOUR YOUNG PERSON'S MENTAL HEALTH

Primarily, listen and take your worries – and those of your young person – seriously. You should never ignore your instincts. Far too many young people are lost to suicide each year and many such deaths are preventable if parents and carers recognise the signs and know where to go to get help. Between 2020 and 2021, rates of suicide among fifteen- to nineteen-year-olds rose by 35 per cent, with the loss of 198 teens in the UK in 2021.[10]

The following are some of the signs that indicate your young person needs urgent mental-health help:

- Increasing mood swings and irritability
- Increasing social withdrawal
- Lack of interest in hobbies and activities they used to enjoy
- A change in sleep habits

- Changing eating patterns
- Paying less attention to their appearance
- Talking about dying, or making death-related art
- Referring to people being better off without them
- Giving away their belongings

If you are concerned about your young person's mental health, please don't hesitate to seek professional help. We wouldn't think twice about taking our young people to the doctor if they had a pain in their chest, yet when the pain is more emotional, we are more likely to hesitate.

Your first port of call, unless it is an emergency, is usually your family doctor, who can refer you to Child and Adolescent Mental Health Services (CAMHS), although there is likely to be a long wait. You can also reach out directly to adolescent mental-health charities (if there isn't one local to you, you can find details of national charities in the Resources section on p. 235). You can also speak with the nurse attached to your young person's school or college, or the student wellbeing services team at their university. If you feel that your young person's health is an emergency and they need immediate help, please never be afraid of calling 999.

Body confidence

As young people grow, they become increasingly concerned about their bodies. Research suggests that up to 90 per cent of teen girls and 70 per cent of teen boys are unhappy with theirs.[11]

Young people today are increasingly exposed to societal ideals of body shape and size, particularly on social media and TV reality shows like *Love Island*. Many feel pressure to conform to these norms and present themselves in a way that they perceive to be desirable to others. In doing so, they put themselves at risk of disordered eating, not only in the present, but potentially for the rest of their lives. Once a young person starts dieting or restricting their food intake, it often leads to a vicious spiral of disordered eating, with research showing that those who begin dieting in adolescence are more likely to become obese in adulthood.[12]

How do we help our young people to escape this slippery slope and embrace their bodies? First, we must be careful to not comment on their bodies, even if we may feel that they have gained a little weight or even lost it. Drawing attention to their changing weight, however well meant, is a known trigger for increasing disordered eating.[13] The best thing to say about a young person's body is nothing. Second, we must be careful about our relationships with our own bodies. Our young people pick up on our body dissatisfaction, and if we say negative things about our own bodies, we can directly influence how they think about theirs.[14]

As with almost everything else we have discussed so far in this book, the solution is unconditional love and acceptance. When our young people feel valued for who they are, they feel much less of a need to try to change.

The idea of unconditional acceptance also applies to a young person's fashion choices. Whether they want to wear bum-skimming skirts, tiny cropped tops, jeans so tight they can barely walk, the waist of their jeans so low that their underwear is visible to all or be covered head to toe in black, it is none of our business. Too many young people have their clothing sexualised and their choices controlled or belittled by their parents, which serves only to dent their self-esteem and make them more self-conscious about their appearance. The same is true of piercings and tattoos. If your young person is old enough to be pierced (most salons and piercing studios have a lower age limit of sixteen) or tattooed (at age eighteen), then their choices really are none of your business. Their body, their choice.

Toxic masculinity

'Be a man', 'Man up', 'Stop being such a girl', 'Why don't you grow a pair?' Phrases like these are all too common in our society today. Toxic masculinity – the pressure for males to possess stereotypical masculine 'strong' traits and no stereotypical 'soft' feminine ones – is hurting our young people. It makes them more afraid to share their emotions for fear of being judged not 'manly' enough, more likely to grow up with poor mental health, and it can cause issues with relationships, romantic or otherwise.[15]

Boys and men do cry. They have feelings and their home should be a place where they feel safe and encouraged to share them. There is nothing unmanly about experiencing sadness, anxiety, frustration, disappointment and grief. Emodiversity is good for everyone. We need to make sure that our sons know this, especially in a world where popular influencers, such as Andrew Tate, become famous for their macho, misogynistic views (more on this in Chapter 8).

If you have a son and haven't yet had a discussion with him about toxic masculinity, this is your sign to do so now. Make sure he knows that adopting clichéd male stereotypes doesn't make him more masculine, just as displaying stereotypes more commonly described as feminine will not make him less masculine. Our young people need to feel free to be themselves, to wear what they want, experience all emotions and behave in a way that feels authentic, not following a narrow set of rules, perpetuated by influencers, podcasts or reality TV shows.

Empowering your son to break free from the constraints and emotional harm caused by toxic masculinity not only helps him but his future partners, too, and even his future children.

Introversion and young people

Introversion is often seen as an undesirable trait in our society, especially in young people. We often label introverted young people as 'shy', 'quiet' or 'withdrawn', and invest far too much time and energy trying to encourage them to come out of their shells. School parents' evenings are great examples of this – I can't tell you how many times I've heard 'they need to speak up more in class and get more involved'. This may sound like sensible advice at first, until you realise the teacher is basically asking the young person to stop being an introvert. All too often, introverted young people feel as if they are somehow failing at developing social skills, which can understandably dent their confidence and self-esteem. Instead, they need to learn that everybody is different – some of us are introverts, some of us are extroverts and both are absolutely fine.

So if you suspect that you are raising an introvert, what can you do to help them embrace who they are and not feel embarrassed? Here are my best tips:

- Don't view introversion as a personality flaw. It is not a problem that needs to be fixed. Rather, it is much easier and far healthier for the young person to accept their personality and see the positives. An introvert often possesses heightened empathy and intuition, great imagination and an analytical mind. They also tend to make good listeners and often have a great deal of focus as they grow.
- Acknowledge that you cannot force the introversion out by pushing your young person to do things that they don't want to do. Forcing a shy young person (however well meant) to go and speak to others, order their own food or pay in a shop will not make them

less shy. Flooding them with exposure will instead likely make things worse, increasing any social anxiety. Give your young person opportunities to branch out on their own if they feel confident enough to do so, but be there to support them (and never pressure) if things don't feel right.

- Focus any verbal praise on effort, not outcome, especially in social situations. Instead of clapping and cheering when they do manage to speak to somebody, or put themselves in the spotlight, focus instead on the tiny moments when they were brave, regardless of whether they 'succeeded' or not. The time they put up their hand in class when the teacher asked a question but put it down again before they were chosen to answer is just as valuable (if not more so) than the time they stood up and spoke in front of a room full of people.

- Make sure that they know you love them unconditionally and that you're proud of them, exactly as they are. Introverted young people can struggle with their self-esteem, so need to know, as often as possible, that you think they are wonderful.

- Explain the difference between introverts and extroverts to them and help them to understand that there are all types of personalities in the world and that none of them is wrong or undesirable.

- Stand up for them and speak out if others tease or berate them for their introversion, especially other family members. Those small moments when your young person feels understood and protected by you will make a huge difference in the future.

- Help your young person with some stress- and anxiety-management techniques, so that they have something to help them cope if they find themselves in unavoidable anxiety-inducing situations. A simple breathing technique, visualisation or fiddle toy (even just a hair band on their wrist to twiddle) can really help.

- Build some quiet time into your young person's schedule. Introverts need time away from others to recharge. Don't be tempted to fill up all weekends or the whole summer holiday with busy activities; allow some days for free time at home, with plenty of opportunities for art, music, reading and writing, and all-important solitude.

This list is also applicable to young people who are on the autistic spectrum, particularly girls (who we know often display very different symptoms to boys) and those who are prone to masking.

Helping young people with a lack of confidence or low self-esteem

Before we end this chapter, I thought it would be a good idea to have a little recap of some of the ways in which we can help our young people if they are struggling with low confidence levels or low self-esteem. There are no quick fixes, but there are many ways in which parents and carers can help.

Unconditional acceptance

Home should be a safe place for your young person to be themselves. Remembering Maslow's hierarchy of needs (see p. 47), in order for a young person to have good self-esteem and confidence, their physical and psychological requirements must first be met, to provide a strong foundation. These include the need for nutritious food, warmth, sleep, a sense of belonging in their family, and unconditional love and acceptance from their parents and carers. Focusing on these basics and plugging any gaps helps to build strong roots from which confidence and self-esteem can bloom.

Embrace mistakes

When your young person is ready to try something new, or perhaps retry something they have not yet mastered, it's important to allow them to make mistakes. It might be tempting to help them by issuing a full set of step-by-step instructions, or to finish tasks for them that they find difficult or frustrating, but doing so can undermine their confidence. Here, the role of the parent is to sit with the young person's frustration and provide them with a sense of self-belief. Remember the FAIL acronym we discussed earlier (First Attempt In Learning)? It applies very much here. Mistakes are inevitable in life and are an important lesson for young people to learn in their quest for improvement. It is only when they successfully navigate problems with as little input from us as possible that their confidence in themselves will really build.

Encourage intrinsic motivation

What should you do when your young person achieves something they have previously found difficult? Conventional wisdom would be to reward them handsomely, with verbal praise and chants of 'well done' – perhaps also a little treat, special meal or cold, hard cash. Ironically, however, rewards such as these can undermine confidence. If your young person is intrinsically motivated to do something – that is, if they are internally driven to do something for no reason other than because they want to – they are more likely to be successful. Too much praise and material rewards foster extrinsic motivation, encouraging young people to do something solely for a reward, the result being that they feel good because of the reward and the praise, not because of their own actions. If we want to encourage confidence, the rewards should always be internal. A sense of mastery, pride, achievement and an increased sense of self-worth can only come from within.

Be careful what you role model

As a parent, you are a role model for your young person. They will look to you to decide how to behave and react in certain situations. It is therefore important that you keep confidence in yourself. If you fail at something, don't say, 'Oh, I'm so stupid'. Instead, say 'I've tried so hard to do this. I'm sure I'll do it one day soon, but today isn't the day.' Your young person needs to see you try and fail as much as they need to see you succeed. They need to know that you make mistakes, just like them, and they need to see you be easy on yourself when you do.

As parents and carers, we can often struggle with feeling not good enough, we doubt our parenting abilities, criticise our looks and are generally pretty down on ourselves. Our young people are constantly looking to us to know how to behave. If we want to raise young people who are accepting of themselves and have good self-esteem, we have to start with improving our own. In many ways, working to raise your young person's confidence is just as much about raising your own.

Lose the labels

Try to avoid labelling your child, especially with words like 'shy', 'nervous' or 'difficult'.

No matter what we think, our young people are always listening to us, and they take our words to heart, which increases the potential for us to damage their self-esteem even more. You could use this to your advantage, however, by allowing them to overhear you saying lots of lovely, positive things about them. Or perhaps let them know directly: a quick text message saying, 'You're brilliant, I love you!' can really help to lift their spirits.

Act as an external regulator for your young person's big feelings

As we know already, young people's brains look different to those of adults. While we are able to think rationally and logically and control our emotions, young people are still developing these skills. Knowing that they can rely on us to 'contain' their big emotions and help them to calm down and make sense of the world when things feel overwhelming, enables them to become more confident in everyday exchanges with the world and those in it.

Become an emodiverse family

Embracing the idea of emodiversity and encouraging all emotions in your home allows your young person to be authentic. This is especially important for young people who are neurodiverse and may spend a lot of time masking in the outside world. They won't feel the need to hide their feelings with you or be on their best behaviour, which means that they won't internalise their feelings, or bury them inside to fester over time. Remember, don't take words they've said in the throes of big emotions to heart. Instead, look for the feelings underneath them – be the adult, take a deep breath and respond to the emotional need. Young people don't have 'attitudes'; they have big emotions which they often find difficult to express and regulate.

Encourage, but don't push

Our young people need us to encourage them to branch out a little and explore more of the world and all it has to offer. Many parents and carers are tempted to push their young people into activities and experiences that they think will be good for them. However, this push will only cause them to feel less confident, not more. Instead, focus on supported, gentle encouragement, at your young person's pace. Encouraging them to take baby steps outside of their comfort zone may feel frustratingly slow, but you'll cover more distance that way.

Listen to the little things – especially at inconvenient times

Listen to your young person's fears and worries and avoid being dismissive of them, especially at times when you're busy or tired – because those are the times when young people seem to need us the most. Rather than saying, 'You'll be OK; don't worry!' say, 'I understand you're worried. That's OK. I feel worried about new things, too. How can I help?' This helps young people to feel validated and to know that they can always share their concerns with you, which will help to improve their self-esteem.

Don't confuse introversion with a lack of confidence

Introverted young people often thrive in quiet environments, with fewer people around. They may prefer to spend time at home, with one friend only, or even alone. This is not a flaw that needs to be fixed and it doesn't mean they are struggling with confidence. Helping them to understand introversion and what it means for them is key here. Showing your child that you love them unconditionally for who they are and not trying to change them is always the best way to help those who are introverts.

It is natural to worry about your young person if they are struggling with low confidence, mood or self-esteem, but what parents and carers need to do is to harness that worry in ways that will help not hinder their young people. Too often, in our quests to 'make them more confident' we can undermine our young people's feelings and make things worse.

There are no quick fixes or magic wands here (just as there aren't with any other aspect of raising young people, in case you haven't realised by now), but with time, patience, understanding, support and unconditional love, your young person will start to bloom – which is a good place to leave this chapter and begin the next, because it is all about behaviour, discipline and boundaries, for which you will need oodles of all five.

Chapter 5

Boundaries and Discipline

*The biggest communication problem is we do not listen
to understand. We listen to reply.*
STEPHEN R. COVEY, American educator and author

This quote sums up the very best advice I could give you
about tackling behaviour problems with your young person.
So much of the discipline advice given to parents and carers of
young people (and also to those who teach them) centres on
trying to 'fix' them. We focus heavily on attempting to train
young people to behave in a more sociable, respectful way, with
tools aimed to disincentivise bad behaviour and motivate the
good. The problem with this approach is that it simply doesn't
work. If it did, I'd wager you probably wouldn't be reading this
book now. We also wouldn't hear parents, carers and teachers
complaining so often about the behaviour of young people, with
constant complaints that 'the teens of today have no respect'.

As Covey's quote above suggests, so many people forget to
listen, and rather than seeking to understand young people and
the causes of their behaviour, they instead focus entirely on
trying to change them.

The best starting point in tackling any behaviour you don't

like from your young person is to understand it. Once you have that all-important understanding, the next step involves focusing on your own conduct and changing it, because it's much easier to control that than your young person's. Only when you blend understanding, empathy and an emphasis on how you yourself behave can you genuinely work to improve your young person's behaviour for the better.

Being the adult

Having raised four young people, there is not much I haven't had to tackle behaviour-wise. Nevertheless, and despite being a so-called 'parenting expert', I've often found myself shouting, dishing out warnings or punishments, or trying to cajole better behaviour from my young people through the use of bribes ('If you tidy your room, I'll pay you'). You see, it's all too easy to slip into the angry, shouty-parent shoes while throwing out increasingly ridiculous consequences. When you find yourself in this state (because, let's face it, everybody does at some point) you can almost guarantee that your young person's behaviour won't improve; instead, they'll join you in a dysregulated-behaviour state, throwing a slightly more grown-up version of a toddler tantrum. And the more you shout, the less they'll listen. The more you try to punish, the more they'll push back.

When you find yourself in this state, you have completely lost control – of yourself and of any chance of changing your young person's behaviour. This rage is a horrible state to find yourself caught up in, because deep down you know it's futile and it also makes both you and your young person feel terrible.

I wonder if you can remember your parent, carer or teacher yelling at you, threatening all sorts of unpleasant things if you didn't do what they asked of you. If you can recall a similar scenario, ask yourself if their behaviour made you more or less likely to comply? Did it make you feel heard? Or understood? Or did you feel you were misunderstood and mistreated? We all know that making young people feel bad doesn't improve their behaviour; the only true solution is understanding and supporting them, so that they feel better – because when they feel better, they behave better.

As I discussed at the start of this book, this understanding means parents need to 'be the adult'. It may sound silly, but often we don't act like adults in these situations – it's almost as though we regress to our teenage selves. But as hard as it is (and boy is it hard), we have to take a deep breath, exhale as much frustration as we can and remind ourselves: 'I need to be the adult here'.

Being the adult means engaging your frontal cortex, drawing on your mature executive functions and working to regulate your emotions, in order to help your young person regulate theirs. When you act as the adult, you remind yourself that you are the one with the mature brain development and it is up to you, not your young person, to diffuse the situation. Being the adult means encouraging emodiversity (see p. 72), embracing mind-mindedness (see p. 74) and reminding yourself that young people don't 'misbehave' for no reason – there is always an underlying issue triggering the big, out-of-control emotions, and it is your job to uncover the real cause.

I have previously spoken about being a role model for children when they are younger. If you want to teach your toddler to say 'please' and 'thank you', you should always express gratitude yourself, especially when your toddler is watching and listening. If you want your five-year-old to learn good table manners, then you must always ensure you sit up straight at the table, elbows by your sides, hold your cutlery correctly and always keep your mouth closed when you chew. Children learn what they see every day. They become who *we are*, not who we want them to be. And this role modelling doesn't stop being relevant as your child grows and enters their teen years. They are still watching you, still listening to you and, most importantly, they still mimic you. If they grow up in a house where the adults resolve conflict through swearing and shouting, then that's what they will learn to do when they fall out with their friends, partners and even you. Once again, you cannot control your young person's behaviour, but you can control your own, and the more you do so, the more likely it is that your young person will behave in positive, sociable and respectful ways.

What if you can't control your own behaviour?

When I work with parents and carers of young people, I always struggle a little with how to break the news that while they may want me to give them advice to change their young people, what they actually need is some advice on how to change themselves.

Everything starts with us. The problem is that it is insanely hard raising young people. Personally, I'd go back to the broken nights of babyhood and the tantrums and fussy eating of toddlerhood in a heartbeat. The issues that felt so huge ten or twenty years ago now seem relatively minor and easy to tackle. Life with young people, as wonderful as it is, often feels overwhelming, with issue after issue, worry after worry. As we get older as parents and carers, we face more issues in our own lives – elderly parents, health concerns, money worries, big career decisions, changing friendships and the stresses of trying to juggle a million 'life balls' at once. Another thing I don't think we discuss enough is how the perimenopause and menopause seem to coincide perfectly with our children reaching adolescence. When both mothers and their young people are going through huge life changes at the same time (something we will discuss much more in Chapter 10) it can lead to a bumpy ride.

All the 'stuff' we are going through takes up headspace, and often it's just too much. Our worries, concerns and frustrations build and then our young people come along and swear at us or refuse to clean up after making a sandwich and we explode at them. When we take some time later to 'be the adult' and calm down, we realise that our response was completely over the top, given our young person's behaviour. We often act as if they have murdered somebody, when all they have done is refused to put their clean washing away. This overreaction is known as 'emotional displacement'. In essence, we are like a volcano, bubbling away, and one small infraction from our young person triggers an eruption, with smoke and boiling magma flowing everywhere. The problem is, when we enter a state of emotional displacement like this, we make everything worse, because our young people explode right back at us.

How do you prevent emotional displacement? The answer is both simple and incredibly hard. You have to make some headspace and, importantly, recognise when you're nearing your limit. When you feel the stress and tension rising, you need to ask yourself: 'How can I offload some off this, so that I don't get so full that I explode?' Very often, this involves learning to say 'no' to people, especially if you're a people-pleaser and find yourself taking on all sorts of tasks that people have asked of you because you're worried they won't like you or will somehow think less of you if you don't. Perhaps you need better boundaries with work colleagues, friends, your partner, if you have one, ex-partner or other family members. Perhaps you need to slow down a little and accept that you're not superhuman. Or perhaps you need to accept that doing a task to a 'good-enough' standard is far more feasible than aiming for perfection. Whatever it is that you personally struggle with (and we all struggle with something), working hard to lessen the burden and create some headspace is the best tool you have. As I said, everything starts with you, and as hard as it is to always have to be the adult, it is really the only thing that works.

Resetting expectations

'They're so full of attitude!' 'I can't believe what I've raised, she's so rude!' 'He's so immature – it's like he deliberately does stupid things for attention.'

What do these three statements have in common? Each one tells us that the person uttering them is expecting too much of their young person. Talk of 'attitude', antisocial behaviour, immaturity and lack of impulse control is effectively just a description of a young person's developing executive functions and emotion-regulation skills. While a lot of their behaviours are undoubtedly incredibly frustrating, most are also completely normal and common for their age. The trouble is, when we expect conduct that is significantly more mature than a young person's neurological capabilities, we're only going to be disappointed when they 'fail' to behave in the expected ways.

The focus of the first four chapters of this book was on learning to understand young people – their needs, their thoughts and their actions. Maybe you wondered why I was starting there, rather than jumping in and focusing on hot topics such as screen time, homework or relationship woes? My whole ethos when working with parents and carers, regardless of the age group they are seeking help with, is based on fully understanding what is happening in the child or young person's brain and how this impacts their behaviour. Because whether we're talking about baby sleep, toddler tantrums, child eating or, indeed, pretty much anything that happens during adolescence and early adulthood, we have incorrect expectations of behaviour. Life would be so much easier for both young people and those who work with and care for them if we actually understood them.

Resetting expectations according to what young people are truly, genuinely capable of, while working hard to 'be the adult' are essential tools for getting through these years with as little stress as possible. Of course, there are little finishing touches and titbits that will make things even easier, but it really does all come back to expectations. Simply, if you expect too much from your young person, you are going to be disappointed. So the next time you feel yourself getting angry with them, try reminding yourself to keep your expectations realistic. Alongside this, try to reframe their behaviour in light of your new expectations, as follows:

- Instead of 'attitude', think 'struggling with emotion regulation'.
- Instead of 'selfishness', think 'developing empathy skills'.
- Instead of 'lack of commitment', think 'identity searching'.
- Instead of 'disorganisation', think 'developing executive functions'.
- Instead of 'laziness', think 'adolescent circadian shift'.

Reframing behaviour is incredibly powerful. It allows you to be more mind-minded, more welcoming of emodiversity, more patient, and it helps you to be a better role model. You will not find a quick fix for your young person's behaviour, but you will understand it more and be in a better headspace to handle it.

Do you really want obedience?

While it may be tempting to imagine life with an amenable young person who does everything you tell them to do and never answers back, obedience isn't all it's cracked up to be.

A young person who is always compliant is probably one who has low self-esteem and confidence and feels unable to speak up for themselves, living a life in which they mask their true feelings. We should also be careful to not just aim for superficial obedience and compliance from our young people, because all that teaches them is to be good liars. For example, if you suspect your young person has done something that you prohibited and you ask them, under threat of punishment, if they have done it, a superficially obedient young person is most likely to lie and say, 'No, I haven't'.

Interestingly, emphasis on obedience has decreased significantly over the last three decades. The World Values Survey (a large-scale look at social values that has taken place regularly since 1981) found that only 12 per cent of UK parents believe that obedience is important today, significantly down from responses in the 1998 survey, in which 50 per cent of parents felt that it was.[1] Parents today place hard work, determination, imagination and independence above obedience.

Does it mean, therefore, that you are permissive and don't discipline your young person if your focus is not obedience? Absolutely not. It just means that you have realistic expectations of them and understand that, sometimes, what is easiest for us is not always best for them.

Why punishment doesn't work

So many people think that discipline from secondary-school age onwards should be about 'tough love' and that treating young people harshly is in their best interest. It isn't. Yes, the world is a harsh place, but punishing, shaming and constantly chastising young people doesn't help to set them up for 'the real world', for two reasons.

First, they already live in the real world. Their childhoods and adolescence weren't a mere practice for adulthood – they have experienced and witnessed plenty of harshness already. Second, if we really want our young people to grow to be confident and resilient, the way to achieve this is not through harshness but through nurturance. I refer you back to Maslow and the need for belonging, love and acceptance (see p. 47). Indeed, those young people who act the 'toughest' – those constantly getting into trouble for physical fights and worse – are usually those who are the most desperate for love. Nurturing parenting from early childhood through to adolescence can help prevent the develop-ment of violent tendencies in the late teens and early twenties.[2,3] It is those young people who struggle with a lack of support and acceptance at home who are more likely to be violent and behave in antisocial ways. Being gentle isn't being soft, nor does it raise 'out-of-control' young people.

When we punish our young people for behaviour that is often outside of their control, we don't motivate them to behave better, and we certainly don't teach them *how* to behave better. All we do is teach them that we are not a safe place for them to express their emotions. Taking away gaming consoles, grounding and removing their freedom, and withholding pocket money for younger teens are all incredibly ineffective because none of them looks for the root cause of tricky behaviour. Instead, they ignore neurological capabilities and serve to fracture the parent–young-person relationship. As adults, we know that if somebody belittles us or treats us in a way that we deem unfair, we don't feel motivated to improve. And the same is true for young people. Research has shown that the harsher the punishments that parents of young people use, the worse their behaviour is likely to be.[4] Punishment simply doesn't work, but nevertheless it remains the mainstay of most discipline advice today.

Why bribery doesn't work (at least not for long)

Research shows us that young people are more sensitive to rewards than both younger children and adults, with activation in the area of the brain responsible for rewards (the ventral striatum – see p. 38) increasing during adolescence.[5] Young people thrive on the dopamine 'high' that rewards create, which is also the reason why they are so risk seeking. In theory, therefore, bribery should work well to encourage better behaviour. In practice, however, it's a little more complicated.

Rewards may be useful in the short term in education settings to temporarily increase motivation in young people to study. They can also be useful (but only on an infrequent basis) if you want your young person to do something they don't want to do and you need a quick response. They become far more problematic, however, when it comes to trying to change behaviour in the long term, which includes behaviour in education.

When we are talking about lasting change, rewards fall flat because they don't consider the cause behind the behaviour. They don't look at whether what is asked of the young person is realistic given their neurological capabilities and, perhaps most importantly, they don't work in the long term because the appeal wears off. If you do resort to bribery often, you will find that it gets more and more expensive over time, because while it may be easy to bribe a five-year-old with stickers, young people tend to want cash, takeaways or expensive clothing and shoes. Aside from the issues with superficial results, it's not sustainable to be constantly paying your young person to do the things you want them to do.

So how do you change the behaviour of the young people you struggle with? As ever, there are no quick fixes, but the most effective discipline techniques centre on the following:

- Starting with realistic expectations of what your young person is capable of
- Being a great role model
- Understanding why they are struggling with a particular behaviour
- Working with them to find solutions
- Having grace and being the adult when things still don't work out as you hoped

Building trust

If you want your young person to come to you with their problems and trust you to help them work through them, you have to make them feel safe with you. This means you shouldn't punish them for what they tell you, otherwise they won't confide in you about their mistakes again. Young people need to not be scared of telling you the truth, however difficult it is for you to hear it. If they do open up to you and you punish them, then you're simply teaching them that it's better for them to lie to you next time.

So how do you build trust with your young person? No matter how hard it is, you have to try not to be judgemental. All young people make mistakes (I'm sure you made plenty of bad choices in your teens and early twenties – I know I certainly did!). When you find out about these mistakes, the response that helps to build trust is to let your young person know that the choice they made wasn't a great one, but you'd like to help them out of any resulting difficulties and help them to make better choices in the future. This isn't about hiding any anger or disappointment – remember, emodiversity is good – but it's about trying to stay calm, being the adult and reminding yourself that, more than anything else, your job is to support your young person to find a way through the difficult situation they find themselves in.

Communication here is also incredibly important. If you want your young person to be truthful and honest with you, then you have to be that way with them, too. This means not trying to shield them from what you yourself are going through, by which I don't mean unloading your problems on to them but answering questions honestly. Working on your own communication skills will help your young person feel more able to open up to you. One of the most powerful phrases I heard when I was younger was: 'You have one mouth and two ears for a reason: listen more than you talk'. The next time your young person is clearly struggling with something and they start to open up to you, remember: 'one mouth, two ears'. All too often, we rush in with advice and instructions for how to solve our young people's problems, when all they need is for us to just listen to them. In the same way that we need to make headspace to avoid exploding with emotional displacement, so do our young people, and staying quiet and listening to them as they offload is so much more helpful than diving in trying to fix things for them. Over time, this technique will help your young person to know that they can always come to you with anything that is worrying them.

Boundary setting

'But isn't all this permissive? Aren't you just letting them get away with everything?'

I hear this a lot when I talk about discipline during adolescence. And I think that's because the approach I take, one of gentle parenting, is constantly misrepresented in the media. Similarly, many people who were raised in a more traditional way, with harsh punishments, cannot comprehend that other, kinder ways of disciplining are effective. So many people from older generations tell me: 'In my day I would have been sent to my room with no dinner, or had my mouth washed out with soap if I spoke to my mother like that!' They think that parenting today is too 'soft' and this 'namby-pamby pandering' is 'what's wrong with teens today'. I do understand where they are coming from. They are wrong, however, and what they are doing is voicing conditioned beliefs about how grown adults should hold a position of power and authority over young people. Theirs is the generation who still believe young people should act with blind obedience and 'respect' towards their elders. What they don't realise is that the 'respect' they speak of is actually fear. Nobody respects somebody who treats them badly. Respect can only truly be gained when somebody acts in inspiring, kind and empathetic ways. The way to genuinely gain respect, therefore, is to be mind-minded and work *with*, not against, our young people.

Are the teens of today out of control? While many would have you believe this is true, it simply isn't. Research shows that today's young people are perhaps the best-behaved generation ever.[6] They are kinder, exhibit more prosocial and less antisocial behaviour, are less rebellious, less violent, more concerned about the environment, achieve more academic qualifications, smoke less, drink less and have fewer teen pregnancies than those before them. To all intents and purposes, they really are much better than our generation and others before us.

Setting boundaries, or house rules, is important for every member of the family, not just young people. You probably already have many, even if you don't realise it. For instance, taking shoes off when you enter the house, tidying up after yourself in the kitchen and keeping quiet at night when others have gone to bed. Some boundaries are based around safety (for instance, not leaving a lit candle in the house if you go out), while some are set out of respect for others (say, putting the toilet seat down after you've finished) and some are set out of personal preference (such as asking your young person to text you, so that you know they've arrived somewhere safely). Clearly, boundaries that involve safety are non-negotiable and always need to be upheld by everybody. Non-safety-related boundaries fall into the desirable but not absolutely necessary category.

Setting boundaries simply means thinking about the non-negotiable and desirable actions that everybody in your home needs to follow, and making your family aware of them. Ideally, though, young people will be involved with boundary setting because discussions will help them to understand the need to follow the rule. Too often, we have arbitrary boundaries which young people don't follow simply because they don't know why they're important. Involving them in discussions and encouraging them to add to your family rules helps them to form a sense of belonging and ownership, which means they are far more likely to stick to them. Sometimes it can help young people if family rules are printed out and hung up in prominent areas of the home – for instance, reminders about changing toilet rolls and hanging up wet towels can be stuck to a bathroom mirror, reminders about turning off the oven, putting empty cartons in the rubbish and cleaning up after making a snack can be stuck on your fridge, and reminders to tidy their room, bring down used cups and plates and rubbish can be stuck on their bedroom wall. This may seem a little over the top, but visual reminders can really help young people while their executive-function skills (see p. 30), particularly working memory, develop.

What should you do if your young person breaches a boundary?

Well, that's entirely up to you. Remember, though, boundaries exist to teach young people, and nobody learns well when they are yelled at, shamed or punished.

My first step when a boundary is breached is always to start with a calm conversation with the young person asking them why they did – or didn't – do something. Sometimes there is a very good explanation; often, the response will revolve around them forgetting or having poor time-management and organisational skills, which is still a pretty good explanation if you consider their neurological development. It's actually quite rare that there is blatant, conscious defiance. If there is, then this is a sure-fire sign that your young person is feeling disconnected and dysregulated, in which case my focus would move from the boundary itself to the emotional needs underlying their behaviour. We can be too fixated on 'the rules' and all too often miss the real problems beneath them.

Once you've uncovered the cause, it's time to put on your adult hat again. You are the one with mature self-regulation, communication and rational-thinking skills. Your young person is not going to learn if you dish out random consequences, especially if you are out of control when doing so. Instead, it's time to have a conversation about why the boundary is important, why it was set in the first place, what your young person can do if they feel that they cannot stick to it and what they can do to try to repair things a little after they've broken it. It really is only after these supportive, non-punitive conversations have taken place with a lot of patience and understanding on your part that you will see the positive change that you hope for.

One last little note here: as we've seen, your young person is still a young person with a young person's brain. They absolutely are going to forget to do things, be disorganised, procrastinate and lose control of their emotions, because they cannot be better than their current level of neurological development. As always, having realistic expectations of their capabilities when you set boundaries is the best route to not being disappointed when your young person breaks them.

How to deal with common, everyday behaviour problems

Often, the issues I'm asked for help with by parents and carers of young people are not serious. Rather, they're everyday niggles – behaviours that in and of themselves aren't dangerous but chip away at the parent's or carer's ability to stay calm. These constant, low-grade frustrations can stack up, one upon the other, causing emotional displacement when the adult can't tolerate them any more. Then starts a vicious circle of out-of-control emotions, anger and frustration, with both parties treating each other disrespectfully.

Learning how to tackle these everyday niggles, then, is really important. My suggestion here is to start by being curious: ask questions, mostly of yourself, but a few to your young person, too. That curiosity will help you to build a fuller picture of their behaviour, helping you to cope with, if not remove it.

The questions that I'd suggest starting with are:

- If they are breaching a boundary, does your young person know why that boundary exists?
- Does your young person understand how their behaviour impacts you and others?
- Do they understand the safety implications of their actions?
- Do they actually know how to do the task that you're asking of them?
- Do they struggle with getting started? Is the task overwhelming them as it is?
- Are your requests of your young person reasonable and appropriate for their neurological development?
- Are you expecting your young person to be more mature and better behaved than even you, as an adult?

- Are you being a good role model?
- Have you tried working collaboratively with your young person to try to solve the issue together?
- Have you actually listened to your young person's concerns?
- How is your connection with them? Has it become a bit fractured recently?
- Are you 'being the adult'? Or do you need to take a breath to calm down?
- Is there something else – a deeper problem – underlying the presenting issue?

It is always important to keep the last point in mind. While you may be arguing with your young person about not replacing the empty toilet roll and their rude attitude when you raised the issue with them, they may actually be 'stroppy' because they have fallen out with their best friend. It doesn't matter how much you talk to them about respecting others if they are feeling like the bottom of their world has fallen out.

How to deal with explosive behaviour

How should you handle explosive behaviour from your young person? What if you or they or somebody else is in danger because of their actions and you need to de-escalate things quickly? Or you find yourself drawn into a yelling match with them?

The first thing to consider here is that if your young person is this out of control, they are incredibly dysregulated and strug- gling to control their emotions. This usually happens because of emotional displacement, meaning that they are bringing far more to the situation than you may at first think. In short, something else – something pretty big – is happening in their life. Maybe you're already aware of it; often you won't be.

What they really need from you when they are this out of control is for you to share your calmness with them, so that they feel safe and can begin to relax. Young people can often get stuck in the 'fight' mode of the fight-or-flight response – full of adrenaline and cortisol, ready to fight for their lives, without realising that their behaviour is irrational or excessive. When they are like this, telling them to 'calm down' is likely to make them a lot worse. All you can do here is to move to keep yourself safe (including putting space between the two of you, so that you can work on your own emotions and calm yourself down), move fragile items away so that they do not get broken, keep younger siblings and pets out of the way and give your young person space, while letting them know (concisely – they won't be able to listen to long statements when the red mist of fight mode is still around them) that you're in the next room to support them if they need you. When you've given them time to calm a little, pop back and ask if they'd like a hug or a chat, or if they'd prefer for you to give them more time and space. It's important you don't try to force a hug or conversation on them if they're not ready for it. It will only backfire.

When they (and you) are calm, then you can discuss what happened with them. Make it clear that you don't want to chastise or punish them; you just want to know what happened and what caused the explosion because you want to help. At this point, you need to remind yourself, as well as your young person, that it is you and them against the problem, not you against them. The two of you are united on one team. Remember 'two ears, one mouth' (see p. 100): ask them if they want you to advise them or just listen. When they do start talking, stick to one issue at a time, don't add in everything else they've done that's been irritating you, dragging stuff up from the past. This is a time to stay firmly in the present while you focus only on the current issue (and any underlying cause). Listen, support, investigate and work together to try to uncover the causes of their behaviour and any potential resolution.

If you find yourself too angry or stressed to do this in the heat of the moment, make it clear to your young person that you need space to calm down, so that you can help them. You could say something like, 'I'm too angry to discuss this right now – I need to calm down first. Can we talk later tonight?' Remember, you need to bring your adult thinking and calmness to the conversation, so if you need time to be able to do that, it's much better to be honest with your young person. After all, honesty builds trust and now, more than ever, your young person needs to trust you.

When communication breaks down

If your young person is acting in ways that are especially un-pleasant, it can be hard to have a calm conversation with them, especially if it feels like the final nail in the coffin at the end of a tough week.

Sometimes young people and their parents and carers find it hard to move beyond the initial backchat, criticisms, squabbles and name calling. In this case, it's better to take a break and pick up on the conversation when you've both had a bit of space. Alternatively, moving the conversation on to paper, a text message or email can be really helpful. Being able to write down your feelings without being misconstrued or spoken over is very healing for both you and your young person. It also means that you can go back to their words and read them again to make sure you've fully understood before being tempted to reply. Young people will often find it easier to open up about big issues they've been worrying about in writing, rather than face to face, especially if it's something they find embarrassing. You could even set up a little notebook between the two of you in which you write notes to each other if you know you will find the conversation more difficult in person.

The importance of rupture and repair

I'd like to end this chapter with the idea of rupture and repair or, as I call it in my book *How to be a Calm Parent*, 'holler and heal' – because regardless of how wonderful a parent or carer you are, how hard you work at staying mind-minded and respectful or how amazing your young person is, there will be a time that you will lose it with them. You will yell, you'll say things that you regret and do things that you're later ashamed of. None of this means there is a problem with you, or that you've failed your young person in some way. It just means you're human. Raising young people can be exhausting mentally, and when we're exhausted and overstretched, we're far more prone to snapping. So I write this section not with the idea of *'what if* you lose it?' but *'when* you lose it'.

The first thing to do in the aftermath of yelling at your young person, dishing out unreasonable punishments or saying something that you know hurt them is to realise that nothing is irreversible. You can absolutely fix this, and indeed, the worst thing you can do is to do nothing, pretend it didn't happen and try to sweep it under the rug. These things don't disappear, but they do fester and eat away at both us and our young people. So own it. Be the adult. First admit to yourself that you screwed up, regroup, take a big, deep breath, calm yourself down and then tell your young person that you were wrong. Admit that you made a mistake – you overreacted and they didn't deserve that response. This doesn't mean that what they said was OK, or that their behaviour was acceptable, but it does mean that they didn't deserve your response. Let them know that you love them and that you are sorry for yelling, saying hurtful things or imposing unfair punishments. The beauty of this is that not only are you ensuring that your relationship with your young person stays strong, but you are also teaching them how to apologise and make things right when they themselves slip up in their relationships in the future. Can you imagine how much better our world would be if all adults could do that?

When you have made things right with your young person and freed yourself from the burden of guilt that far too many parents and carers carry with them, it's time to reflect on the situation. What could you have done differently? How could you have worded something better? How can you work to respond to your young person's underlying emotional needs, rather than react to their superficial behaviour in the future?

I firmly believe that no parent is perfect. Nobody knows all the answers (especially not me) and we never stop learning and growing as parents – there is always something we can do better and something that we can learn from situations. As much as rupture and repair, or holler and heal, is about making things right with your young person, it's also about forgiving yourself and using the situation as a period of reflection for personal growth.

I hope this chapter has helped you to understand your young person's difficult behaviour a little more, and given you some ideas for tackling any concerns or niggles that you may have. In Chapter 11, I answer thirteen of the most common behaviour- and discipline-related questions I am asked by parents and carers of young people, giving more specific advice about how to handle certain scenarios. My answers, however, always come back to the same five points:

- Checking your expectations are realistic
- Considering how your young person feels

- Checking your own behaviour
- Working collaboratively to resolve issues
- Healing any rupture in your relationship with them

If you follow these steps, they will see you through almost any issues you may have.

To conclude, here is a statement that I hope you will take to heart and think about often, especially if you find yourself doubting how you have behaved towards your young person in the past: it's never too late to repair a relationship or treat your young person with more empathy and respect.

Chapter 6

School and Education

We worry about what a child will become tomorrow, yet we forget that he is someone today.

STACIA TAUSCHER, Irish artist

I wonder what your experiences of education as a young person were? Did you love every minute of learning and embrace the opportunity for further study at college or university? Or could you not wait to leave school and start a job as soon as possible? Perhaps you struggled with a special educational need or found it difficult to conform and behave in ways that were expected of you?

I fall into the first category and look back on my school years fondly. I took the traditional route of GCSEs, A-levels and then a degree. I don't regret for a minute the academic path I ended up taking. If I could go back in time, I wouldn't change anything. That doesn't mean I was a perfect student, though; nor does it mean my parents didn't have any struggles with me. I learned very quickly that I was a very capable student who could get away with doing the bare minimum of work and I would still pass everything. I spent the entirety of my GCSE study leave hanging out with my friends, going shopping and watching movies, and didn't revise at all for my A-levels. Consequently, my results were much lower than predicted for almost every subject. I was supposedly a 'straight-A' student, but walked out of my GCSEs and A-levels with a large haul of Cs. I passed my degree with a 2:1 – a respectable grade – but I could definitely have scored a first if I had prioritised my studies over the student night club and bar. Do I regret my lack of motivation to be the best I could be? Absolutely not. I managed to achieve what I wanted, and I had a lot of fun doing it. I was 'good enough' as a student and, importantly, I was happy and am happy now.

Their future, not yours

One of the hardest things about being a parent of a young person is learning that you have to let go of any hopes, wishes and dreams you held for them about their future. You have to understand that they are your dreams, not theirs. You have to accept that they are their own person with their own choices, which probably look very different to those you hoped they would make. While you may hope that your young person will leave school with high grades and pursue higher education, they may not want to, even if they are academically gifted. You may be excited that your young person is capable of top grades, but the worst thing you can do is push them to try to achieve them. They are more than their grades, they are more than their education record and their future is not yours to decide. As a mother of four young people, I understand how hard this is. We enjoy being proud of our young people and want the best for them, and many of us have fallen under the spell of believing this is only possible if they excel at their exams. But this is just not true.

If you are a user of X (formerly Twitter), and venture online on GCSE or A-level results day, you probably will have come across a now infamous post from Jeremy Clarkson that states: 'It's not the end of the world if your A level results aren't what you'd hoped for. I got a C and 2 Us and here I am today ...' followed by a different ending each year, including 'with a brewery', 'with a Mercedes Benz', 'sitting in a villa in St Tropez' and 'on a superyacht in the Med'. In a blog on the Virgin website, business-man Richard Branson talks about his experience with dyslexia at school and how failing his exams and dropping out of school at sixteen didn't hold him back in life, saying, 'Your grades don't define you, and there's so much more to life beyond the school gates'.[1] Billionaire businessman Lord Alan Sugar has only one O-level (the equivalent of one GCSE today) and dropped out of school before his A-levels to start Amstrad, the business that earned him a fortune, when he was only twenty-one. Record executive and TV personality Simon Cowell dropped out of school at sixteen, too, also having passed only one exam, while multi-million-pound business owner and 'Dragon' Deborah Meaden never completed her A-levels. It may feel as if your young person's future career choices and life options will be severely limited if they do not excel at school, but these people and thousands more are proof that exam results do not define who you are and who you can become.

The importance of failure

I often give speeches at large blue-chip companies, city banks and huge international law firms. Naturally, these offices and auditoriums are full of extremely high achievers, earning huge salaries. The parents who attend these talks often have teens at private or selective state grammar schools and are keen that their children should excel, so that they can get into Cambridge or Oxford University. Understandably, they are worried that their young people are not taking advantage of the opportunities offered to them and they often ask me how they can make their young person revise more and work harder, or simply 'take things seriously'. My answer is always the same, regardless of where the young person goes to school and what their parents' dreams for them are, and is summed up in three words: let them fail.

You can imagine how well this advice goes down. It's usually met with protestations of 'But what if they fail everything?', 'What if they can't get into university?' and 'But what if they don't get the grades they need for a good career?' Still, my advice never wavers. Letting a young person fail is the most powerful way to encourage them to take some responsibility for their learning, to help them to dig deep and find out what it is they want to do in life and to motivate them to work harder if an academic route is what's needed for their chosen career path.

When your young person was a toddler and they tried to touch the oven door, you would probably shout 'Stop! It's hot! Don't touch, it will hurt you!' and inevitably your sweet little chubby-cheeked toddler would then reach out, touch the oven door, and cry 'Owww!' They didn't listen to you because they did not have the neurological capacity to fully comprehend the repercussions of touching the oven door. Your now grown young person most likely thinks that they are invincible, not because they have a personality problem, but because of the 'personal fable' we learned about when we discussed identity development (see p. 53), and they also struggle with hypothetical thinking and immature executive functions. They are not really much different to the little toddler they once were. It doesn't matter how many times you warn them of the dire consequences of not doing their homework, not revising and not taking their education seriously – they will only truly learn when they experience first-hand the repercussions.

When your young person goes to school and hasn't done their homework, they will get a detention or similar. When they sit an exam they haven't revised for, they will feel a sinking feeling in the pit of their stomach as they turn over the first page and realise that they can't answer anything. When they pick their exam results up and see a sea of low grades, and don't get into their first-choice university or lose an apprenticeship they had lined up, they will finally understand why you warned them that studying should come before their social life. This may sound harsh, and you may be thinking, 'Really? You're suggesting I let them screw up the rest of their life?' But I'm not. Statements like these are overdramatic. They have plenty of time to resit exams, take a gap year, apply for new jobs and courses, and work out who they are and who they want to be in the world of work. They may not end up on the timeline and in the places you had planned for them, but that's OK. They will find their own path and it will be far more suited to them and something they are much more likely to stick at if they are motivated to pursue it. Adolescence and the early twenties, when young people are able to live at home, are the safest years to screw up and start all over again. There is no better time to learn about failure.

Homework woes

'How do I get my young person to do their homework?'

This has to be in the top five questions I am asked about teens and schooling. The idea of homework is a contentious one. There is no straightforward answer about whether it is 'good' or 'bad' for learning at secondary- or high-school level. Usually, the efficacy boils down to the type of homework that is set and what its purpose is. 'Good' homework focuses on young people consolidating learning and is used in such a way that a teacher can assess students' understanding and knowledge in order to tweak their lessons. 'Bad' homework is set with little thought given to learning objectives and outcomes and is done simply as a 'tick-box' exercise to appease governing bodies and inspectors. It's not your young person's fault if the homework is of poor quality, resulting in a lack of motivation to complete it. Sadly, with the amount of pressure placed on teachers who work in underfunded and understaffed schools, homework often falls into the latter category because they just don't have the time or the resources to provide truly meaningful homework. Time spent on completing work outside of school also matters. Research has found that the optimum amount of time spent on homework during adolescence for the best academic outcomes is about one hour per day.[2] If your young person does significantly more than this, it is too much, and you should speak to the school about reducing it.

The way schools tackle homework compliance is also debatable. If a young person doesn't complete their homework in time, sanctions usually kick in and they quickly find themselves given a detention. However, research shows that if young people only complete homework to avoid punishment, either at school or from parents, then their engagement with learning and their motivation to study are negatively impacted.[3] Similarly, it may be tempting to be highly controlling and force your young person to do their homework, perhaps under threat of removal of privileges, but research shows this approach backfires, too. Young people with parents who have a high level of control over homework tend to achieve lower academic results.[4]

What is the answer, then?

We need to help our young people to develop the skills needed to work autonomously, setting them up to succeed by helping them with the following:

- **Providing the right environment to study** Do they have a quiet, clutter-free space in which to concentrate? Do they have the equipment they need?
- **Helping them to get into a routine** For instance, when they get home from school, having a snack,

then a brief rest, then on to homework before they access screens. It's incredibly hard to get off screens, given young people's drive towards rewards and the dopamine high that screens provide, so explaining this and why it's better to get their homework completed first helps.

- **Helping them to organise themselves** Remember, a young person's executive-function skills aren't mature, and they will struggle with time management, prioritising tasks and procrastination. Drawing up a study planner with them, blocking out time and presenting it visually, with step-by-step timings can help to get them started.
- **Checking that they understand why they are doing the homework** Too often, young people believe there is no point to the homework (sometimes they're not wrong!), and that teachers are on some sort of personal vendetta to destroy their lives (definitely wrong!). When they understand the purpose of homework, they are usually a little happier to complete it.
- **Checking they know exactly what they have to do** Sometimes quickly scribbled words in a homework diary are vague and young people are reluctant to start because they don't know exactly what they're doing. Encourage them to check with their teacher, if there is any confusion.
- **Making sure that they aren't struggling too much with the work** If young people are confused, or don't understand the work they have been doing in class, they will obviously find homework much harder. Commonly, however, they won't tell the teacher they don't understand in front of their peers because they are embarrassed. If they are struggling, encourage them to speak to the teacher. If this is a recurring

pattern, contacting the teacher yourself or raising it during a parents' evening is important.

- **Making sure that your young person isn't overscheduled** It's great when they want to take part in after-school activities (it's also fine if they don't), but sometimes they can be overstretched and shattered and not have enough time or energy for homework.
- **Considering alternative times** Some young people really need the evenings and weekends to relax and discharge. If their school offers a homework club at lunchtime or immediately after school, they may do much better to get the work out of the way there, leaving home solely as a place of relaxation.

Picking up on one of the points in this list, that of checking that your young person knows exactly what to do for their homework, this is something that I missed with my eldest young person and had to learn the hard way. He came home from school on a Friday evening and told us he had to 'make a volcano' for school on Monday as part of his Geography GCSE homework. He said he had decided to make his from papier mâché and wanted to include an internal chamber that held baking soda, to which he would add white vinegar and red food colouring at school, to create an eruption. This volcano took over our entire weekend, causing huge amounts of stress and tension in our home. Nothing else got done, only volcano construction, with my husband and I busy trying to find and purchase all necessary craft items and lava ingredients, clearing space in the home for the construction and keeping younger siblings and pets out of the way. By Sunday night it was finally complete, mounted on a 2m² board, covered in fake grass and moss, with trees taken from my husband's boyhood train set. The volcano itself was over a metre tall and painstakingly painted. Monday morning came and because it was impossible for our son to walk to school with the volcano, my husband had to start work late so he could drive him in. Monday evening came and the first thing we all asked when he came home from school was 'Did your teacher like the volcano? What did she say?' He went very quiet and then said, 'Yeah. She liked it.' After more probing, he said, 'We actually had to draw a diagram of a volcano and colour in the separate sections, but I don't think I was listening properly when she told us what to do. She was a bit surprised when I gave my homework in.' The moral of this story is always to check that your young person knows exactly what they need to do if their homework seems to take too long or seems short notice given the amount of time they have to complete it. We will never get that weekend back!

Support during exams

The question that often follows 'How do I get my young person to do their homework?' is usually 'How do I get them to revise for their exams?' As with my answer to the homework question – unfortunately you can't *get* your young person to do anything, especially not revision. What you have to do, once again, is to don your adult hat and ask yourself what is getting in the way of their revision? Aside from neurological development and still-maturing executive-function skills, that is. When we look at what is holding young people back, then we can work with them to help solve any problems they have.

Some questions I would consider are as follows:

- **Do they actually know how to revise?** This sounds such an obvious question, but it's one that is seldom asked. It's rare that schools teach revision techniques in any depth; usually, they are jumbled together into a quick assembly or a one-hour PSHE (personal,

social, health and economic) class. This really isn't
enough. The art of revision and finding techniques
that work for you takes time. Teachers may recommend
a mind map, but this doesn't work if you struggle
with abstract-thinking skills. They may recommend
mnemonics, but again, if your working memory is
still developing, trying to remember the mnemonic
itself is difficult enough, without having to try to
remember what each letter stands for. Making endless
piles of revision cards is tedious and particularly
problematic for those who struggle with attention.
BBC Bitesize may be a brilliant resource, but the pull
to sneak in time on TikTok or Snapchat while online
is often too much for those with little impulse control.
What young people really need is to fully understand
all the different techniques available, enough time
to practise them without the pressure of looming
exams, and support from adults to know where to get
started. Revision is such an overwhelming task for
many students and they can get so panicked that they
don't even start – because doing no revision is far less
stressful for them.

- **Do they struggle with the subject matter?** There is
little time for teachers to make sure that all students
understand all topics within modern curriculums.
Governments are forever adding more content, and
teachers and students are increasingly stressed trying
to cover it all. Naturally, some get left behind and, for
whatever reason, they don't tell anybody that they're
struggling. If they haven't understood part (or parts)
of the curriculum, then by the time they're meant to
revise they may be having to teach themselves whole
topics, or substantial parts of them, from scratch. This
is overwhelming for young people, and without an

adult identifying the problem and supporting them to find solutions (such as attending catch-up sessions at school, if available), they tend, again, to ignore the problem and hope it goes away.

- **Do they have time to revise properly?** Does your young person have enough time to fit revision in? If they spend all weekend working and maybe attend clubs or after-school activities, then when are they meant to revise? Similarly, if their work is making them exhausted, they are either going to prioritise sleep or won't be able to focus.

- **Are they getting enough sleep?** Picking up on the last point again: perhaps your young person doesn't have a job, or perhaps they only work a few hours a week, but if they are up all night gaming, chatting with friends online or meeting up with friends 'in real life' every night, it's likely they aren't getting enough sleep. It is common knowledge that many young people are sleep deprived and that sleep deprivation significantly reduces academic attainment. They don't just need enough sleep the night before an exam, they also need enough sleep in the months running up to it, when they are revising. We'll talk a little more about optimising your young person's sleep later in this chapter.

- **Are they struggling with anxiety?** Most of us will get anxious about exams, but for some young people the anxiety is overwhelming. Sometimes they put too much pressure on themselves to get brilliant marks; sometimes the pressure comes from us, the parents and carers, or sometimes their teachers. Often, all three. Some young people will struggle during exams because of neurodivergence and sensory issues when they're actually in the exam hall. Some will already be tackling anxiety and the added stress of exams can be more than they can hold at times. Here, the two most important things you can do are to let your young person know that you support them and that you love them unconditionally. Let them know that they are not their grades – they are so much more – and what matters most to you is that they are healthy and happy. Take off the pressure at home. Speak to their form tutor, the school's SENCO (special educational needs co-ordinator) or its pastoral team and ask for some support and alternative exam arrangements, such as taking them into a separate room from the rest of their cohort. You can also work with your young person to help them find some breathing or mindfulness techniques to use 'in the moment' when they're feeling overwhelmed.

- **Allow them to fail.** As we discussed earlier in this chapter, one of the most powerful ways we can encourage our young people to understand the importance of revision, is to allow them to fail their exams. Most schools will have tests well before the all-important ones happen (usually end-of-term or end-of-year tests) and most students will sit at least one, if not two, rounds of mocks before their GCSEs and A-levels. These practice tests are the perfect chance to allow your young person to fail. When they get into the exam hall and realise that their blasé attitude was a mistake or they get their results and it becomes clear that they are miles away from what they need for the next step in their education or career, they are far more likely to be motivated to improve for the real thing than with any amount of chastisement and lecturing from you.

Is it a good idea to pay young people for good exam results?

Perhaps you were given a certain amount of money from your parents or carers when you received your exam results? The practice was common when I was at school and still is today. Some of my young people's friends received in excess of £1,000 for their GCSEs – a mind-blowing amount of money that is simply unaffordable for most families. These young people were promised £100 for every A grade (or a 7, 8 or 9, as the new numerical system works), £75 for a B (or a 6), £50 for a C (a 4 or 5) and £25 for a D (a 3). My young people were obviously keen for us to do similar.

While this approach may seem clever at first, it comes with numerous problems. The first is obvious: in a cost-of-living crisis, most can't afford to pay their young person to study. The second is that this approach is based on extrinsically motivating young people to study – they do it simply for the cash and this does nothing to help them to develop an innate motivation to study because they want to better themselves. And the problem here is that once you start this bribery, you need to continue it with any other courses and exams they pursue. That's a lot of cash over the years. The final problem is that if you have more than one young person, this approach is not fair to siblings who are less academically gifted or who have special educational needs. A neurotypical, naturally academic young person who achieves an A without too much effort does not deserve more of a reward than a young person with ADHD, autism or dyslexia, who struggles hard at school and through a huge amount of effort has managed to get a D. In fact, if your reward was based on effort, the D would be rewarded with significantly more cash than the A.

For all these reasons, I agreed with my own young people, that we would give them a flat rate of £20 per GCSE, whatever grade they got, not as a reward, but as a celebration for completing them, giving them a bit of cash so that they could go out and enjoy themselves with their friends. If you choose to do similar, then obviously the amount you give is dictated by your household budget. It is also absolutely not wrong to give nothing – instead, you could celebrate with their favourite home-cooked meal with a friend or similar.

Disruptive behaviour in school

Many young people struggle with their behaviour in school and too often they are punished with strict sanctions, which do nothing to help with the cause of their behaviour. I do understand how difficult a job teachers have (my eldest is one and we have had many conversations about student behaviour and how tough teaching is), but 'zero-tolerance' approaches to behaviour at school are a step backwards in academic pedagogy. Behaviour-control methods involving shaming, punishing and socially excluding young people may appear to work superficially, but when you consider what 'work' actually means, it throws up many moral questions.

If a behaviour-control method 'works', most involved in education say things like: 'They're easier to teach', 'The class is less disruptive', 'They're quieter' and 'I can cover the topics I need to get done'. Some schools will tell you that their behaviour policies 'work' because of their outstanding exam results or Ofsted inspections (though what they don't tell you is that very often the 'difficult' children are told to stay at home on the day of the inspection). What these claims don't consider, however, is how the policies 'work' for the young person. Do they 'work' to improve their mental health? Do they 'work' to support their learning disability? Do they 'work' to improve their motivation to study? Do they 'work' to resolve any problems they are having at home which are affecting their ability to behave at school? The answer here is that all the 'zero-tolerance' behaviour policies that 'work' do so for the staff and not for the young people in their care – or certainly not those who are struggling anyway.

If your young person's behaviour is getting out of control at school, the first question you need to ask is 'Why?' Why are they behaving like this? Why can't they concentrate? Why are they being disrespectful towards staff or their fellow students? There is always an underlying reason for the behaviour. Many who are supporters of the zero-tolerance approach ridicule the idea of 'all behaviour is communication', but I think they misunderstand what is meant by 'communication' here. All behaviour has an underlying root cause, which is indisputable. Sometimes that cause is incredibly hard to find; sometimes you can never find it. But what is true is that no young person consciously chooses to deliberately be disruptive at school if all is well in their world. Adding more punishment on top without finding the cause is, at best, completely pointless.

So what are some of the whys behind difficult behaviour at school? The following are just a few:

- Neurodivergence and SEND (special educational needs and disabilities), often undiagnosed
- Being a victim of bullying
- Struggling to understand and keep up in lessons
- Struggling to hear or see properly in lessons
- Friendship problems
- Trauma or stress at home
- The impact of poverty
- Sleep deprivation
- Lack of positive role models at home
- Lack of parental support
- A medical condition affecting how they eat or sleep

This list could be endless and, just like adults, all young people carry 'life stuff' in their buckets and when they are too full, they overflow. Emotional displacement (see p. 93) is an extremely common cause of difficult behaviour at school. If you look at the list on the previous page, I hope you can see that detentions, isolations, exclusions and failing to achieve rewards are all ineffective at helping to fix the underlying cause of difficult behaviour. The only way to make real change is to play investigator, ask 'Why?' and work with the young person to help them to feel better, so they can behave better.

SEND, SUPPORT AND THE LAW

In Chapter 1 we learned that 28 per cent of young people with autism don't receive a diagnosis until they are at secondary school. ADHD is similarly underdiagnosed, especially for girls. If you suspect your young person is neurodivergent, or that they may have another special educational need, such as dyslexia, please trust your instinct. Book an appointment with your family doctor or a meeting with the school SENCO and keep pushing until they listen. I speak from experience of fighting the system for a decade, until I was finally taken seriously and given some help for my son who has ADHD. His diagnosis came just before his GCSEs and life at school would have been much easier for him – and for his father and me – had he been diagnosed earlier. Not necessarily because the school could have offered him more support (they probably couldn't, because SEND is woefully underfunded and most schools barely scratch the surface of what young people with SEND need), but because once a young person has a diagnosis, it is much easier to stand up for them.

If a child with a disability, who uses a wheelchair, is unable to compete in a school running race, they do not receive negative behaviour points or a detention or isolation. If they did, the school would be in breach of the 2010 Equality Act. Why, then, do so many discriminate against those with neurological-based conditions? A child with ADHD who is constantly in detention for forgetting homework or not paying attention in class is simply being punished for their ADHD, which is discriminatory and illegal.

The Equality Act states that education providers must not directly (for example, refusing admission) or indirectly (for example, by not providing suitable adjustments) discriminate against students with a disability.[5] Students with a disability must not be harassed by teachers or school staff (for example, being shouted at for not concentrating in class if their disability causes them to struggle with concentration) and they should also not be victimised (for example, if they complained about the shouting teacher and received a suspension because of speaking out). The school should also provide reasonable adjustments for all students with a disability, ensuring that they have the support they need (whether physical or emotional, such as support from a teaching assistant) in order to thrive. Clearly, schools that punish young people who have autism, ADHD or other SEND for symptoms of their condition are in breach of this act.

What young people with SEND need more than anything from us as parents and carers is for us to be their advocates. To stand up for them and their legal rights, to challenge the school's treatment of them, to ensure that they get the 'reasonable adjustments' that they are legally entitled to and to always be in their corner. As a parent, it can feel as if you are constantly fighting a system designed for round pegs when your young person is a square one. We shouldn't have to, of course, and the system certainly needs overhauling, with the rights of young people with SEND centred, but we are still a long way from this. Budgets are too low and understanding of the needs of young people with SEND in education, particularly from those in government, is still lacking. The fight is draining and, sometimes, it feels as if you are wading through treacle backwards, but you have to keep trying. When the going feels too tough, the best thing you can do is to reach out to support groups and charities who help young people with SEND and their families, particularly when it comes to knowing your legal rights (see Resources, p. 235).

We can also help our young people to be as informed as possible about their condition and how it affects them at school. When young people have such a rough ride at school it can really dent their self-esteem, so we need to help them to realise that they are more than a diagnosis and that they are loved unconditionally for exactly who they are.

Bullying in school

Bullying is shockingly common, with 40 per cent of young people having been bullied in the last year. Heartbreakingly, 6 per cent say that they are being bullied on a daily basis.[6]

The most common type of bullying, making up 26 per cent of all incidences, involves name-calling and verbal abuse, both online (via texts and social media) and in person. The second-most common type, comprising 18 per cent of all cases, is social exclusion, when young people are pushed out of friendship groups. Thankfully, physical bullying is relatively rare, but it does still happen.

Bullying, especially unchecked, can have catastrophic consequences for a young person's mental health and academic achievement and their perception of their own academic ability, especially if the bullying is prolonged.[7] Many young people who bully others are victims of bullying themselves, sometimes at home, by those who should love and care for them the most. Others are led to bullying because of difficult social relationships, trauma, poor self-esteem and mental-health issues. While it is likely that those doing the bullying are also experiencing something themselves, it doesn't mean it's OK to bully others.

Not all young people share with their parents, carers and teachers if they are being bullied, so it's important to know the signs, which may include the following:

- Seeming more anxious or withdrawn than normal
- Not wanting to go to school
- Not spending time with their friends as they used to
- Having more emotional-displacement outbursts at home
- Exhibiting more difficult behaviour at school
- Being angrier and ruder to siblings than normal
- Declining grades and achievement at school
- Loss of interest in hobbies and activities
- Spending more time alone in their room
- Visible marks on their body, or damaged clothing or other property
- Any other behaviour which seems out of the norm for them

How to support your young person through bullying

- Listen to them – this is definitely a time for 'one mouth, two ears' (see p. 100).

- Ask them what they want you to do about it. Don't immediately rush to the school if that's not what they want you to do.
- Help them to understand why bullying happens. Explain that it's very unlikely to be about them, but rather what the perpetrator(s) is going through. This doesn't mean that they should forgive them, but it does mean that they can understand that they are not being bullied because of an inherent problem with themselves.
- Ask them to keep a diary, noting what happened and when. This is especially important if you want to raise the issue with their school.
- Check in with them regularly and ask how things are going. Don't wait for them to come to you.
- Make your home their safe haven. Be extra aware that they need to feel a sense of support and belonging at home, now more than ever.
- Plan some fun activities and time with them, not to take their mind off the bullying (which is unlikely to happen), but to give them something to look forward to.
- Give them some tools and ways to respond at the time of the bullying, such as a specific phrase they could say to the bully. For instance 'I don't appreciate it when you speak to me like that', or simply 'please stop!'.
- Encourage them to form a new group of friends, especially if a friend (whether current or past) is instigating the bullying.
- Help them to identify a trusted adult in school who they can go to during the school day if they need to talk, or just want to feel safe and supported.

Unless the bullying ends quickly, it is very likely that you will have to get your young person's school involved. Initially, you should contact their form tutor or head of year. If your young person is diagnosed with a SEND, then also speak to the SENCO. Ask to see their anti-bullying policy and make sure your initial contact is in writing, also taking notes during any meetings and asking the school to email you the main points discussed and their plan. If the bullying is not resolved after these meetings, then escalate to the deputy head or head teacher, and if there is still no resolution, take a formal complaint to the board of governors. Again, make sure this is in writing, as it then has to be stored and may be read during an Ofsted inspection. This tends to make sure it is taken seriously.

Finally, some forms of bullying are illegal, such as that involving racism, homophobia, transphobia and other forms of hate speech, as well as physical attacks. If you believe that a crime has been committed you could also consider contacting the police, especially if it is not quickly dealt with and stopped by the school.

THE IMPACT OF COVID ON YOUNG PEOPLE IN EDUCATION

While our memories of the Covid pandemic lockdowns may be fading, the impact is long-lasting, especially for our young people. So many of them missed important transitions and life events when they were confined to their homes during the spring of 2020 and again in the autumn and winter of that year, with school buildings remaining closed for most pupils. In total, young people lost around half a year's worth of face-to-face teaching because of lockdowns.

Research has found that young people from high socio-economic groups lost a total of 21 per cent of learning, while those in the lowest groups were much worse hit, with a loss of 34 per cent.[8] But it wasn't just the effect of lost learning time that young people struggled with – they were not able to see their friends or romantic partners, they missed Year 7 and Year 12 transition days, they missed eighteenth-birthday celebrations, driving lessons, proms, first jobs and going in to school to pick up exam results with their friends. All things we took for granted in our teen years. And there are young people studying at university now who are facing taking exams for the very first time, after their GCSE and A-level exams were scrapped and they were given predicted grades in their place.

During the summer term of 2022, so-called 'ghost children' – those who were missing for at least half the term – numbered over 140,000 in the UK.[9] There are still an alarming number of young people not engaging in education today. The pandemic took a huge toll on the mental health of young people and the effects are lasting. It is not excessive to consider that the school-related effects of lockdowns will last for at least another decade, while those who were in infant and primary school during the pandemic grow and enter their teens. Parents, carers and teachers of young people must remember the impact of the pandemic whenever they are talking about any problems that young people of this generation experience at school.

School refusal

While Covid has had a massive impact on school attendance, it is not the only reason for increasingly high rates of young people who do not go to school. While many call this phenomenon 'school refusal', this makes it sound like deliberate defiance but, of course, it isn't remotely this simple. A more accurate term is 'emotionally based school avoidance' (EBSA for short), which helps parents, carers and school staff alike to realise that young people who do not attend school are not just being stubborn, defiant or 'naughty' (as many mistakenly believe), but that there are complex underlying wellbeing and mental-health reasons. For some, EBSA can mean that they are completely unable to attend school at all, whereas others are able to go, but regularly skip lessons, hiding somewhere on school grounds, while still others attend, but infrequently.

Punishing a young person for EBSA or attempting to bribe them to attend school with rewards is unhelpful. Just as we discussed in the previous chapter, carrot-and-stick approaches ignore the underlying causes of a young person's behaviour and do absolutely nothing to help resolve the difficulties they are facing. Similarly, some schools jump straight into a process of 'systematic desensitisation' or graduated exposure therapy, where young people are encouraged to attend school for short amounts of time, slowly increasing these once they've achieved attendance. This idea can be helpful, but only if the underlying issues are worked with first.

What are the causes of EBSA?

There are a myriad of reasons for EBSA, which are unique for each young person. Often, there is a link with SEND, some sort of trauma, bullying, anxiety and other mental-health concerns. Sometimes no specific causes can be found, but the young person suffers huge amounts of psychological trauma when they go to school or even engage with things related to it, such as their uniform.

While EBSA is an emotional phenomenon, there are often physical manifestations, related to anxiety and stress, such as a tummy ache, headache and nausea. These physical side effects can make the anxiety even worse for young people in a huge negative-feedback spiral.

Working with young people with EBSA needs a collaborative approach, which involves the school (especially the SENCO), sometimes external mental-health support providers and, most importantly, listening to your young person. Ideally, you will all come up with a plan together that is regularly reviewed and is one that your young person contributes to and feels they have ownership of. The plan should include helping your young person to understand the physical manifestations of signs of stress and to come up with some coping strategies that can help them, including breathing and relaxation techniques, mindfulness and cognitive behavioural therapy (CBT) to work with any distressing self-chatter and automatic negative thoughts related to school attendance. When your young person feels that they are able to begin to engage with school again, then baby steps should be taken, ideally designed by the young person, towards reintroduction. When they are able to attend school, they should have a safe space and a member of staff they trust who they can talk to, if needed.

At home, parents and carers should try to make things as calm and pressure-free as possible. Home is your young person's safe place. Try to keep things organised, sticking to routines which are reassuring, and try to avoid stressful, panicked rushes in the morning before school. More than anything else, being the parent or carer of a young person with EBSA requires you to be the adult. This is not your fault, but neither is it your young person's. Take a deep breath, try to stay calm and remind yourself that your young person's mental health is much more important than academic achievement. With this in mind, sometimes leaving the system is the best answer for your young person. School is not for everybody.

School alternatives

While attending school is the social norm, it isn't the only option available. Some young people just aren't made to be at school, following rules and focusing on a narrow range of academic subjects. These individuals do much better with more freedom, more time in nature and more scope to excel at the things they enjoy – perhaps the arts or construction. For these young people, taking them out of the system and allowing them to flourish in their own unique ways is the best decision (and one made predominantly by the young person themselves, rather than one you make for them).

While there are alternative schools, such as democratic and Steiner schools, home education (home ed) has seen a rise in popularity in recent years, especially after many families had a forced taster during Covid. While a lot of home-ed resources focus on younger children, there are still thriving communities for teens, including many with co-operative set-ups, where parents and carers share their knowledge and local experts are employed to do the same about specific subjects. Young people who are home educated can still take examinations if they wish, and many progress on to sixth form, college and university, while others follow a more entrepreneurial, artistic or trade-based route, without examinations.

If home ed isn't quite for you or your young person, there are also options for online schooling. Once again, Covid lockdowns taught us how to design and deliver an education programme online to best meet the needs of young people, and many new online school providers have developed different offerings. These come with a cost, unfortunately, averaging between £200 and £400 per month, depending on the syllabus followed and the age of your young person. However, if your young person has EBSA and is really struggling to engage, it's worth a conversation with their school to ask if it may be able to provide them with a free online education. Some state schools are able to help with this.

Sleep and studies

We've touched on sleep in this book already, but I couldn't end this chapter without revisiting the subject.

We already know that young people have a different body clock to both younger children and adults, and that this evening chronotype clashes with early school starting times. If those who run the education system valued this information and shifted this time just an hour (to somewhere between 9 and 9.30 a.m.), we would see significant positive changes. Research shows that starting school an hour later means young people get an average of forty-three minutes more sleep each night, which would go some way to reducing the large numbers of them who are chronically sleep deprived.[10,11] Unsurprisingly, sleep deprivation creates more sleepiness in class and more depression, with most young people questioned by researchers saying that they felt they struggled with sleep.[12] A lack of sleep in adolescence also negatively affects cognitive function, and is linked to an increased risk of obesity and metabolic issues.[13,14] The idea of 'catching up on sleep' at the weekend is a myth; in fact, the large difference in sleep and wake times between weekdays and weekends only compounds the issue, leading to more disturbed circadian rhythms.

As parents and carers, helping our young people to optimise their sleep is important in enabling them to feel more settled and reach their potential with their studies. Here are a few simple, realistic tips:

- Keep bright and blue-based lighting out of their bedroom. For the best sleep, encourage them to turn down the brightness on any screens they use in the evening and select bedroom lighting that is red- or orange-based. These are the only light colours that don't inhibit the secretion of melatonin, the hormone of sleep.[15]
- Aim for a cooler bedroom temperature and good ventilation. Research has shown that fresh air in a bedroom increases the length of deep sleep.[16]
- Aim for as consistent a sleep onset and wake time as possible.
- Try to encourage your young person to get outside every day, even if only for a short time. Daily sunlight exposure has been shown to improve sleep quality, and far too many young people spend all day inside.[17]
- Try to encourage a calming bedtime routine. It doesn't have to be long or complicated – just something as simple as switching on a red night light, opening the window, getting clothing ready and bags packed for the next day, and spritzing a sleep spray in the room before getting into bed can help.
- Cut back on energy drinks, regardless of the time of day they are drunk. With over two-thirds of young people regularly having these, the effect on sleep is a concern, especially considering that research shows a link between young people who drink them and getting insufficient sleep.[18,19]
- Reduce caffeine intake, especially in the afternoons

and evenings. Research shows that for the best sleep, coffee in particular should, ideally, not be consumed in the eight hours prior to bedtime.[20]

• Check your young person's diet, especially the amount of iron they consume. Insomnia and related daytime sleepiness have been linked with low iron levels in young people.[21]

• Introduce some sleep aids for your young person to use, for instance an aromatherapy diffuser, a pillow spray or a meditation app.

While we do what we can, as adults, to try to help our young people to improve their sleep, what they need is for their circadian rhythm to synch up with the rest of the world, alongside developing some impulse control and rational-thinking skills, so that they can put their phones down, turn off their PCs, avoid that one last cup of coffee or sip of energy drink and prioritise the need for sleep. The skills needed to reach these decisions, however, are ones that many simply don't possess yet, and so it makes no difference how much we, as adults, talk about how chronically sleep deprived our young people are. Instead, we can aim to take the edge off the sleep deprivation with small changes that they accept, which are enough to help them get through their day at school. It's not ideal, but then there are no ideal solutions. In time, as your young person grows and matures into a fully fledged adult, they will begin to prioritise their sleep, and you – and they – will look back on these testing times with fondness, ready to repeat them with a whole new generation of your family in the future.

Talk of sleep and screens and the tricky habits of our young people is a good place to end this chapter, because the next one covers these, and how to handle them, in detail. As well as screens, we will also talk about alcohol, drugs and the new habit on the block – vaping. If you haven't had to tackle these problems yet, please don't skip this chapter because, at some point, you will, and preparation and prevention are by far the best approach.

Chapter 7

The Internet, Alcohol, Drugs and Vaping

New technology is not good or evil in and of itself. It's all about how people choose to use it.

DAVID WONG, author

We've touched on screens a couple of times so far in this book, noting that they are bad for young people's sleep, which has a knock-on effect on their physical and emotional wellbeing and their academic achievement. Screen time is a hot topic in the world of parenting books, magazines, websites and social media discussion groups. If a daytime television show runs a segment on teenagers, invariably talk will quickly turn to the opinion that screen time is the cause of almost all problems exhibited by teens today. And at least once a month I will be asked to contribute to a news story about 'teen screen detoxes', 'screen-free weeks' and 'how to wean your teen off screens'. Screen time has been demonised in our society, but I for one am not on board with that.

Many are shocked when they hear my opinion, believing that I, as a so-called 'parenting expert', will hold strong 'anti-screen' views. But I don't. Screens are a vital part of life today. We can reminisce all we want about 'the good old days', when we only had three or four TV channels and played outside with our friends from dusk 'til dawn', but the fact is that life has moved on. Those days aren't coming back, no matter how much we pine for them. If anything, screens are only going to become a bigger part of our lives in the future. I do not think it is realistic or sustainable to try to recreate the past and live screen-free, or overly restrict access for our young people. So while I will give you some tips to put screen-time boundaries in place with your young person, I'm not going to add to society's screen demonisation in this chapter.

Four other areas in which it is vital for parents and carers of young people to be well versed are gaming/social media, alcohol, drugs and vaping. We may think we know enough about these subjects based on our own teenage experiences (or current activities), but we don't. Time moves on and so do potential threats to our young people. The way they interact with social media is not the same way that we do as adults. The risks posed to them are different, too, not just because of their developing brains but because of the exposure to strangers. When it comes to alcohol, we must also be aware of our own actions and how these affect our young people, something that is so simple yet so often overlooked. While drugs have always been around, the ones that our young people are exposed to now are different from those that were available years ago. Drugs today are increasingly synthetic, introducing another layer of danger, and while we may prefer to think that our young people can avoid drugs completely, this is not the case, especially if they go to university, where they are rife. Finally in this chapter, we will look at vaping, an entirely new risk that parents and carers are having to navigate for the first time ever. This is difficult enough in itself, with no tried-and-tested advice to fall back on, but vaping is also terrifying as there is no body of historical data concerning any long-term risks. Our young people are the guinea-pig generation for vaping, and we are the first generation of parents and carers to try to navigate the risks and dilemmas that it brings. We'll come back to this idea at the end of this chapter, but for now, let's turn our attention back to screens.

Why screens are *good* for teens

I'm sure you've read a hundred and one reasons why screens are bad for young people. When my youngest young person started sixth form recently, a large part of the parent information session at the start of the academic year was focused on warning parents about the dangers of screen time. While screens obviously bring risks and can damage emotional and physical health (something I think we all know by now), there was not one single mention of the positives of screens. So let's redress the balance a little.

Screen time brings numerous benefits for young people, including the following:

- They help them to form new friends and romantic relationships, which can be incredibly helpful to young people who struggle to form connections in person.
- Screens help them to stay connected with friends they already have, including those who have moved away and now live hundreds or thousands of miles away. The impact of Covid lockdowns would have been so much worse if young people had not been able to stay connected with their friends online.
- Screens help young people to socialise. In a society that provides few socialisation opportunities for them (gone are many of the youth clubs, discos, dances and sneaking into pubs underage from when we were young).

- Screens help young people to plug knowledge gaps when overworked teachers can't cover topics to a level where all students fully grasp a concept. My own young people have managed to understand complex mathematical or scientific ideas they struggled with at school because of Instagram reels or TikTok videos. They also provide great revision tools.
- Screens help young people to prepare for the careers of tomorrow. Who would have thought, ten or twenty years ago, that social media management would have been a job? Now it is a huge industry.
- Screens can help young people to launch their own businesses in a way that is just not accessible to them in person. One of my young people makes an impressive income from 'user-generated content', working as a freelancer around his university studies, designing experiences on a popular gaming platform.
- Screens provide competitive opportunities for young people to join e-sports teams. The connections and team relationships here provide the same benefits as those from a 'real-life' sports team. There is also a huge amount of money to be won, which can help set young people up for life financially.
- Screens can help young people to regulate their emotions, especially those with ADHD and autism. If he's having a tough day, my young person who has ADHD is always calmer after spending an hour or so gaming.
- Used wisely, screens can help young people to increase their confidence and self-esteem by connecting with others, excelling at a game or using social media in a way that makes them feel supported and part of a community.

- Gaming can increase intelligence and prosocial behaviour.[1] Many adults underestimate the skills developed through problem solving and teamwork when playing online with others. Gaming can also help young people to increase levels of empathy and decrease violent behaviour.[2]

Screens can also be a great way for us, as parents and carers, to connect with our young people. Joining them in a game as a way to spend time with them or sending them a text or private message on social media to tell them we loved their post or video are really lovely opportunities for us to join them on their level and engage with their interests. This is something I think many parents and carers could benefit from, especially if they struggle to get their young people to spend time with them.

Am I saying young people should have unrestricted access to screens? Absolutely not! Of course there should be boundaries. With our adult hats on we know that screens can cause issues with emotional and physical wellbeing and can also negatively impact our young people's education, and I think we have a duty to use our mature executive functions to help them to limit these serious negative side effects. I just think we should ease up a little on the 'anti-screen' messages so prevalent today and, instead, try to find a balance. Screens aren't going anywhere; we have to learn to live with them sensibly.

That said, what boundaries would I suggest you put in place around screens? They vary slightly, depending on the type of screen time, so let's focus on the two main ones: gaming and social media.

Gaming boundaries

For young people who choose to spend time online gaming, boundaries really need to revolve around safety and making sure that it does not take over their lives to the detriment of their sleep, health, studies and work. These are my suggestions:

- Encourage your young person to take regular breaks to stretch their legs and to breathe and calm down a little if they are playing a particularly tense game. Setting an alarm to go off every hour or so can help, as time goes quickly when gaming, and although they may be happy to take breaks, the chances are they will forget to do so once they are absorbed in their game.
- Staring at a screen for too long can cause problems with eyesight, causing digital eye strain. This may also make your young person more prone to headaches. So it's a good idea to encourage them to practise exercises for their eyesight. Aiming to look away from the screen and focus on something further away every twenty minutes can help to ameliorate issues here.
- Following on from the eyesight issue above, ask your young person to wear light-blocking glasses if they are gaming in the evening. These can be bought cheaply online and look like normal sunglasses, but they filter out the blue light given off by the screen which is so problematic for sleep.
- Teach your young person to prioritise their homework and revision. Come up with a plan and timetable for fitting in school and college work *and* gaming. Considering the draw of screens, academic work should come first, with the lure of the screen as a reward for

them to get on with the work, knowing they can go online later.

- Help them to prioritise sleep. First, you should explain the impact of screens on sleep. Talk about the blue light emitted and how it tricks the brain into thinking it's daytime (again, bring up the importance of wearing the light-blocking glasses) and discuss the addictive nature of gaming, whereby they will lose track of time and easily miss their body's tiredness signals. Explain that if the game is particularly stressful or makes them feel wound up, it will be hard to relax when they get off, and so they need to allow time to relax before bed – for at least an hour, ideally. Young people will naturally struggle with this, because they lack impulse control, so discuss the use of parental Wi-Fi controls. Agree with them on a time that your Wi-Fi will be turned off each night, explaining that this is not done as a punishment but as something to help them if they're struggling to get off their screens. Encourage them to set a timer ten minutes before the Wi-Fi is due to go off, so they can save their game beforehand.

- Young people often get so involved in a game that they forget to eat. When they do eat, they can be ravenous, as well as eager to get back to the game as quickly as possible. This means they are prone to trying to grab ready-made or 'junk' food, rather than preparing food that will nourish them and, most importantly, fill them up. Teach your young person about the difference in satiety levels these foods provide and why this pattern of eating can lead to health problems and obesity. Encourage them to take regular breaks for eating, perhaps setting an alarm so they don't forget. And teach them to prepare some filling, healthy snacks that they can make quickly.

- Help your young person to notice when they are getting angry or stressed. Talk about feelings in their body, such as tension in their jaw, neck or shoulders, and how these are signs that they should take a break for a bit.
- Finally, it is imperative that you have conversations about online safety. Your young person will, at some point, be playing online with strangers. Those strangers may be the same age as them, with genuine motivations, or they may be paedophiles waiting to groom younger teens, or scammers waiting to take their money. Young people must know the dangers of being online and you must set rules about never giving away any identifiable features, including their real name, the area in which you live, names of pets and schools (or accidentally showing school logos on uniform if they have a camera on). Most importantly, your young person should know that if anybody says anything or asks them to do anything that makes them feel uncomfortable while they are online, then they should come to you.

Social media boundaries

Pretty much all the boundaries I've suggested for gaming apply here as well. I won't repeat them, but I would like to add some that are more unique to social media usage:

- Social media sites all have different age restrictions. Check the age rating for the site or app your young person wants to use and don't be tempted to lie so they can access it. For those with a low restriction age of thirteen, make sure your young person's age is entered correctly, as many sites and apps have added protection for young people based upon their date of birth as registered on their account.

- Make full use of the parental controls afforded by your young person's phone and your Wi-Fi providers. Many will have settings that ban over-eighteen content for those underage, as well as settings relating to gambling, blocking certain sites or even search options.

- Make sure you speak to your young person about how social media affects mental health. It can be helpful, with studies showing that it can have a positive impact on their emotions and also helps provide them with information about how to improve their mental health, but there is also a much darker side.[3] Research shows that social media can become addictive for young people, leaving them feeling reliant on likes, comments and shares to feel good about themselves; it can also increase anxiety and cause low moods.[4] Teach your young person to discern between time spent online that makes them feel good and time that makes them feel bad, and encourage them to try to strike a balance, coming to you if they feel that it is weighted more towards the negative side.

- Talk about disturbing trends online, paying attention to what is happening currently yourself (see Resources, p. 235, to help you to stay up to date). Spaces on social media such as 'pro-ana' (anorexia inspiration) communities are particularly worrying, and dangerous dares, like 'chroming' (where young people film themselves inhaling toxic chemicals, especially via aerosols, such as those from a deodorant), have caused several tragic deaths. Similarly, remember that young people can be exposed to almost anything online, from graphic videos showing death, torture and the impact of war to pornography or sexually explicit images. Again, encourage your young person to talk to you if they come across something that upsets them.

- Urge your young person to take regular breaks and also to take time to read books, watch movies and focus on the world around them. Many young people today are seeing their attention spans – already short because of their age – decreasing, with constant exposure to short reels and TikTok videos. These can be great, but it's important that they don't use them as their only form of entertainment.

- Speak to your young person about online bullying. Research shows that one in eight young people under the age of sixteen has been bullied online. Among young people who have a probable mental-health disorder this figure moves to one in four.[5] It's imperative that your young person understands the harm caused by online bullying, so that they are not tempted to bully somebody else; similarly, if they feel that they are on the receiving end of it, they must know that they can come to you and talk about their experiences. The advice from the previous chapter about bullying in schools applies here (see pp. 128–131).

Social media can bring many positives to young people, and most will engage in its use regularly. Again, I don't think it is realistic to impose a social media ban (you will find they will probably open an account secretly if you do), nor do I think 'digital detoxes' are the answer. Instead it's about us, as adults, being as informed as possible, having honest conversations with our young people and always being there to support them if they need us.

What example are we setting with our own screen-time usage?

I'm often approached by parents when I give talks, who ask me for advice to encourage their young people to use screens less. As they ask, they will be clutching their mobile phones; many scroll through their phones while I am giving the talk. The problem here is that it doesn't matter what boundaries or rules we put in place, how much we talk to young people about the risks involved with screen time or try to reduce the time they spend online, if we, as parents and carers, are not following the same boundaries and advice.

If you would like your young person to use screens less, can you honestly say that you are a good example to them? We often kid ourselves that it's OK that we use screens so much because we're doing it for work, we're ordering food shopping, emailing the school or keeping up with the family on social media. While these are all valid reasons for using screens, they do not justify why there is one rule for us and another for our young people. Simply, if we want to change the way screens are used in our families, we have to start by being the change ourselves.

Young people and alcohol

Young people today have a much better relationship with alcohol than we had during our adolescence. While we may have snuck into a pub at sixteen or got drunk on cans of cider in the park at fourteen, research shows most young people today don't try any alcohol at all until they are fifteen or older.[6] This doesn't mean, however, that alcohol doesn't pose a risk to our young people. In fact, in any given year, around 10,000 young people are treated for alcohol poisoning in hospital in the UK.[7] And those who drink regularly are also more likely to have problems with alcohol dependence as adults.[8]

So how do you help your young person grow up with a healthy attitude towards alcohol? Here are my top tips:

- Talk openly and honestly with your young person about alcohol. Unless you do not drink it for religious reasons, it's best to take an approach that shows you know they are likely to want to (at some point in the future, if they haven't yet) and that you'd like them to know how to reduce the risks, rather than prohibiting it entirely (because they will just drink behind your back and lie to you about it if you do).
- Make sure that your young people are aware of laws surrounding the purchase and drinking of alcohol, especially related to drinking and driving. Regarding the latter, they should also understand that although they may be legal to drive after having one drink, it is best that they remain completely sober. Impulse control means they may struggle to stop after one and their propensity to take more risks than those who are older means that any alcohol will make driving more dangerous.
- Explain the risks of alcohol poisoning to them and teach them how to drink sensibly, pacing drinks and knowing when to stop. Plus, talk about signs of alcohol poisoning (such as losing consciousness, excessive vomiting, irregular breathing and slowed heart rate) and what to do if they notice them – either their own symptoms or those of a friend.
- If your under-eighteen-year-old is invited to a party where you know there will be alcohol, contact the parents of the host(s) and ask them any questions you

need to in order to feel confident about your young
person attending.

- Make sure they know they can always ask you for help
if they have been drinking – whether that's picking
them up if they do not feel safe to drive, if they don't
feel safe to be a passenger in a car if the driver has
been drinking, asking you to pick them up from a
party early or asking for your advice if they are feeling
ill at any time. Again, the key to helping your young
person to feel comfortable asking for your help lies in
them knowing that you will not yell at them, punish
them or make them feel ashamed for their choices.

What example are we setting with our own relationship with alcohol?

Once again, the tables are turned on us. We will not raise young
people who have a healthy attitude towards alcohol if we struggle
with drinking ourselves. And I'm not necessarily talking about
alcohol dependency here, but perhaps turning to alcohol to solve
our stress – for instance, pouring a big glass of wine when we get
home from work and loudly proclaiming, 'I needed that!' This
sends young people the message that alcohol is a healthy and
reliable way to fix stress, anxiety and other problems, when it
clearly isn't.

Similarly, over the last decade or so there has been an increasing trend of making light of alcohol as a way to fix all
adult problems, with a humorous slant. We have books talking
about parental alcohol consumption in a funny light and slo-
gans adorning clothing, greeting cards, gifts and so on, saying
things like 'wine o'clock' and 'gin time'. While we may think
these alcohol-related puns are funny, they again teach our young

people that alcohol is the solution to everything. If we want them to have a responsible approach to drinking, we have to seriously consider the messages they receive from us.

Young people and drugs

Research shows that one-fifth of girls and a quarter of boys between the ages of seventeen and nineteen have tried an illicit drug.[9] I'm not easily shocked but was absolutely dumbfounded at how widespread drug usage is at university when my eldest started. Within a day of him moving into his Russell Group University halls of residence he had received a leaflet posted to his flat from the local dealer. A couple of days later, a different dealer made personal calls to each flat handing out business cards with a QR code which linked to a menu, offering a plethora of different illegal substances which could be ordered via an app and delivered straight to their door like a pizza. My son was also regularly stopped in the street and offered drugs on his walk to and from the university throughout his three years there. A common practice during 'pres' (pre-drinking in your flat before going out for the night, in order to avoid expensive alcohol on a student budget) is for a student household to club together to buy a bulk order of ket (ketamine), spice (synthetic cannabinoids), molly (ecstasy/MDMA), nox (nitrous oxide canisters) or tabs (LSD/acid).

Drugs are a huge part of the university scene, and if your young person hasn't encountered them at school, college or work (which they probably have), you can guarantee they will if they go to university. Research has found that 56 per cent of UK university students have tried drugs at least once, and 39 per cent were still using them at the time of being questioned.[10]

Sadly, it's not a case of *if* your young person will be exposed to drugs, but *when*. With this in mind, it's vital that you have conversations with them about it. Far too many parents leave this to school PSHE sessions, but young people need more; importantly, they must know that they can trust you if they have any questions or need advice. My tips here would be very similar to those related to alcohol (see p. 150), so I won't repeat them. I would say, however, that most parents have poor knowledge of the drugs scene these days. Things have moved on a lot from the cannabis joints of our youth, and today the choice is mind-boggling, with increasingly synthetic offerings added to the menu, often cut with terrifying chemicals and toxic substances, including glass, cement and talcum powder.

Young people today play a lottery every time they take something, not knowing what they are consuming. As parents and carers, we have to be well informed on this. The 'don't-do-drugs' messages of our youth are simply insufficient today. We need to be able to have honest conversations with our young people, making them aware of the risks of drugs, but, most importantly, focusing on the idea of risk reduction if they do come into contact with them. See Resources, p. 235, for contact information to help with this.

COUNTY LINES

All parents should be aware of 'county lines' – a form of drug dealing that utilises children and teenagers. Gang leaders pretend to befriend young people, often those from poor areas, usually luring them in with the promise of cash, a new pair of trainers, a new phone or similar. The young people are then drawn into the gang and made to deliver drugs, with contact via a mobile phone (known as county lines) to places that are usually outside of the town they live in, often in more rural areas. The idea here is that young teens are, theoretically, less likely to be 'stopped and searched' and caught by the police, so they are used to keep the gang leaders safe from personal criminal prosecution. Once young people are involved in county lines, it is incredibly difficult for them to leave, with many increasingly exploited and threatened.

All parents should have conversations about county lines with their young people, starting with explaining the phenomenon and the motives behind the activity of the criminals. Make sure your young person feels safe to talk to you if they are ever approached, and also encourage them to talk to you if they are concerned that any of their friends are caught up in county lines. If they know somebody who suddenly and unexpectedly has money, new clothing, a bike, a games console or an expensive watch, with no real explanation as to where the items came from, encourage them to let you – or a teacher or another trusted adult – know. If you yourself have concerns, then call the police or speak to the safeguarding lead at your young person's school or college.

Young people and vaping

If I were writing this book ten years ago, this section would have been about smoking. However, cigarettes seem to be dying out, especially among young people, which is great news. In 2023, only 3.5 per cent of young people questioned said they smoked (compared to 9 per cent surveyed in 2003), whereas 7.5 per cent said they vaped (used an e-cigarette).[11] The latter figure is rising by about 10 per cent each year. The same survey showed that 20 per cent of young people had tried vaping at least once in 2023, an increase from 15 per cent in 2022 and 14 per cent in 2020. More than two-thirds of young people questioned revealed that their vape of choice was a disposable one.

Vapes work by producing flavoured vapour containing nicotine. The vapour comes from a liquid cocktail of chemicals which include glycerine, propylene glycol, acrolein (usually used as a weedkiller), benzene (found in car exhaust fumes), cadmium (a metal), diethylene glycol (used in antifreeze), flavourings and nicotine. This liquid is heated and the resulting vapour is inhaled.

Vapes were originally intended as a smoking-cessation tool for adults, and they have fulfilled their role well here. However, there is now an epidemic of vaping among young people, who use the vapes recreationally, not as the smoking-cessation tool they were originally intended to be. There are several problems here, the first being the lack of long-term data considering the impact of vaping on the health of young people. The evidence we do have currently paints a stark picture, though. We know that there is likely to be a long-term negative impact on the developing brain, and the heavy metals and carcinogenic chemicals contained in the vapes are probably a ticking timebomb.[12,13] But it isn't only the physical effects parents and carers of young people should be worried about. Research has shown that vaping negatively affects young people's mental health, with those who do it more likely to report anxiety and depression than their non-vaping peers.[14] Developing an unhealthy reliance on vaping can cause a young person to not seek proper help, which can make their mental health worse. Use of vapes also increases the risk of other substance abuse, including traditional cigarettes, cannabis and even cocaine. Young people are also more likely to become addicted to vaping than adults, because their brains are wired for rewards, and this addiction can create a lifetime habit that's difficult to break.[15] Also, a vape only ends when the canister runs out, meaning young people will often take a puff every few minutes throughout the whole day.

Vaping presents a huge moral and political issue. There has been talk of government banning disposable vapes but, at the time of writing, no law has materialised. Unfortunately, the current lack of regulation means that nicotine levels are often far higher than those allowed in cigarettes. Many shops sell illegal imports which have no consideration for health or safety. These vapes contain many toxic chemicals and can also be a fire risk. Due to a lack of marketing controls (like those imposed on the tobacco industry), vapes are aggressively marketed to young people. The actual vapes themselves and their packaging usually use bright colours, with novelty shapes, such as those mimicking highlighter pens or bottles of sports drinks. Their tastes are formulated to be overly sweet, using fruity or candy flavours. While two of the largest manufacturers (Lost Mary and Elf Bar) have said they plan to stop selling candy-flavoured vapes, and the UK Government has indicated that it plans to ban flavoured vapes, at the time of writing there are currently no official bans outside of China, where they are based. The bright colours, sweet flavours and cheap prices (an average disposable vape can be bought for £5) are all aimed at young people, and suck them in.[16] What was meant as a smoking-cessation tool for adults has become a fashion accessory and an addiction for thousands of young people.

Vaping really is the scourge of our times. We owe it to our young people to change things, but the solution has to involve governments, with tighter manufacturing, retail and marketing laws, and until we have these we can only do our best with educating them. My tips here are similar to those that we have already covered in this book, consisting of open, frank and honest communication. We cannot force young people not to vape. It doesn't matter how many times we threaten, punish, yell and prohibit them or confiscate their vapes. The only thing they will really take note of is calm explanation and the example that we set for them. If you vape, then perhaps the best thing you can do if you don't want your young person to follow that example is to give up yourself.

I think it would be a good idea to sum up the general advice we have covered in this chapter. Whether we're talking screens, alcohol, drugs or vapes, there are five points that all parents and carers of young people should consider:

We need to recognise that their world is full of screens, alcohol, drugs and vapes. As much as we would like to, we cannot shield them from these. They *will be* exposed to them, and just telling them 'No, don't do that' is not enough. In fact, it may be the most damaging path we can take, because our young people will just learn to be sneaky, to rebel and to lie to us.

As parents and carers, we need to educate ourselves about the ever-changing risks that surround young people today, so that we can answer their questions honestly. It's important to let your young person know that they can always tell you anything and come to you for advice and answers. If they trust that you will listen to them and support them, then they are far more likely to be honest with you.

Our focus should be on reducing risk, not promoting avoidance. This doesn't mean we condone screen time without boundaries, alcohol or drug abuse, and constant vaping. What it does mean is that we are realistic. Abstinence (outside of religious approaches) is not a feasible goal for many young people. So instead, we should help them to reduce the risks to keep them safe.

We have to be careful what we role model. Our young people are always watching us and listening to us (even though it often doesn't feel like it!). If we have unhealthy relationships with screens, alcohol or drugs, or we vape, then it doesn't matter what we try to teach them. They are going to follow our example. Perhaps this is a sign for us to change our own habits a little?

If you are worried, please seek professional help (see Resources, p. 235).

I understand this chapter has been heavy and, at times, I suspect a little shocking. Although I would love to keep this book as upbeat as possible, I think perhaps sometimes parents and carers do need a little scare. I'm not sure that enough people know some of the very real risks our young people face, often on a daily or at least weekly basis. We can't afford to stick our heads in the sand and try to convince ourselves 'not my son/not my daughter'. As uncomfortable as it is, we have to get informed, we have to understand and we have to work with our young people to try to keep them as safe as possible.

I think I've driven that point home enough for now. And I feel it's time to move on to the next chapter, where we will talk about young love and your young person's friendships.

Chapter 8

Friendships and Relationships

The first time you fall in love, it changes you forever and no matter how hard you try, that feeling just never goes away.

NICHOLAS SPARKS, author of *The Notebook*

As a teen, I attended an all-girls school. If you've ever watched the movie *Mean Girls*, you'll have a good idea of what it was like. We had 'the populars', 'the cool-but-different ones', 'the sporty ones', 'the music ones', 'the drama ones', 'the weird ones' and 'the clever ones'. (I was in 'the music ones', if you're interested.) Rarely did these groups ever mix. School was a sort of weird rivalry between the groups, and everybody knew their place – a little like the 'Class System' sketch with the Two Ronnies and John Cleese (give it a Google, if you don't know the one I mean). I was pretty low down the ranking system, and I was OK with that because I had my friends, and we were happy with our place.

Looking back now, I'm pretty horrified at it all – especially for those in the lowest ranking, 'the weird ones', who were on the receiving end of hideous amounts of bullying every day. Alas, this sort of friendship division is all too common in the teen years, and while some young people have strong friendships that help to support and lift them, many struggle with constant fallings-out and changing friendships. We will begin this chapter with an investigation into young people's friendships, talking about how you can help your son or daughter to navigate some of the most common issues that arise. Then we will move on to talk of romantic relationships and how you might help your young person through good times and bad. This chapter also explores how parents and carers can navigate the tricky issues of consent, sex, contraception, unplanned pregnancy and pornography. The information in this chapter applies to young people, regardless of whether they identify as straight or gay, although you will find some specific information on supporting your LGBTQ+ young person, too.

How friendships affect young people

As you would expect, research has shown how important friendships are during adolescence. A study of over 20,000 reports concerning their effects on young people has shown that there is a correlation between the strength of their friendships and their self-esteem levels.[1] Similarly, young people who have strong friendships report a greater sense of life satisfaction, overall better emotional wellbeing and are happier. Those with fewer or poorer friendships, on the other hand, report feeling lonely and more depressed. Research has shown that strong friendships in adolescence don't just affect mental health at the time, but can also impact it long into adulthood, both positively and negatively.[2] Friendships also correlate with academic achievement, with those reporting at least one close friend achieving higher qualifications than those who do not. Given the impact of friendships on young people, both good and bad, it is unsurprising, then, that most rate a friend in the top three most influential people in their life when asked.[3]

While we may believe that having a wide circle of friends is important to young people, in fact the opposite seems to be true: 98 per cent report having at least one close friend, with 78 per cent saying they have between one and five close friends.[4] Only 20 per cent say that they have six or more close friends. Younger teens, between the ages of thirteen and fourteen, tend to gravitate towards friends of the same sex; however, between the ages of fifteen and seventeen, two-thirds report having a close friendship with somebody of the opposite sex. Only half of those questioned said that they felt they fitted in and made friends easily, with most friendships being forged at school.

How to make – and be – a good friend

While many young people make friends with ease, to some it doesn't come as naturally. What can you do if your young person falls into the latter category?

First, don't automatically assume that they are unhappy and need to make more friends. If you are a social butterfly with multiple friends, who would feel lonely in their situation, it can be hard not to project your feelings on to your young person. But just remember, they are not you, and if they have one good friend, they may be happy with how things are. If, however, your young person is struggling to make friends and they *do* want to change their situation, chatting about how they might find like-minded people and ways to break the ice can really help them.

If your young person is an introvert or neurodivergent, they may find it difficult to approach potential friends and instead wait for others to approach them. This is great if they are taken under the wing of somebody who is more extroverted, but not so great if a potential new friend also struggles in social situations. Helping your young person to understand that others may feel like them, too, and encouraging them to take a deep breath and introduce themselves can help them to get over initial hurdles. If they find this challenging, ask the school if it can help to nurture a friendship with someone who is a good match for your young person. Many schools will have pastoral teams and wellbeing groups or rooms that are intended for exactly this sort of thing. If your young person isn't at school, but attends groups or organised activities, then perhaps you could take the first step and speak to the parent of another young person they get on with to arrange a meet-up.

What does a good friend look like? I asked several young people this question and this is what they told me:

- 'Somebody who cares about you.'
- 'Somebody who still wants to be with you even when you're sad.'
- 'Somebody who makes you laugh.'
- 'Somebody you can be yourself with and don't have to pretend to be somebody else.'
- 'Somebody who has your back.'
- 'Somebody you can tell anything to and know they will keep your secret.'
- 'Somebody you can trust and who trusts you.'
- 'Somebody you know would never deliberately hurt you.'
- 'Somebody who likes the same things as you.'

If your young person does have a friend (or friends) who make(s) them feel stressed or sad with regularity, then talk with them about the fact that friends are meant to lift you up, not put you down, and encourage them to consider if they may be better off looking to make a new friend.

Falling out

It's almost inevitable that young people will fall out with their friends at times. Even the healthiest friendships can have misunderstandings and miscommunications. The key here is helping your young person to know what a healthy (and therefore unhealthy) friendship looks like. Healthy friendships involve trust, boundaries and respect for the needs of both parties. Young people should feel able to say 'no' if they don't want to do something, without repercussions. If your young person feels that they cannot voice how they really feel for fear of upsetting their friend or being on the receiving end of some sort of psychological punishment, then this is not a true friendship. If there is someone who wants to be their friend one day but not the next (especially when there are perceived better options), then they are not a true friend either. If your young person doesn't feel able to trust their friend with their worries, concerns and inner thoughts without them being leaked, then they too are not a true friend. Finally, if your young person's friend makes them feel that they have to change and act in a certain way with them, then they are not a true friend.

Too many young people believe they are in a friendship but have to give in to the wishes of the other person, masking their true feelings and living in fear of being ditched at any minute. If the friendship goes wrong, they will often blame themselves and mistakenly believe that they are somehow the problem. We have to help these young people to realise that there is nothing wrong with them, but rather the issues lie with the person they have chosen to be friends with.

While most young people would recognise physical or overt aggression (including hitting, punching, pushing and kicking) as being a problem in a friendship, many struggle to identify covert or relational aggression. Relational aggression includes gossiping, spreading rumours, coercion, gaslighting (a form of psychological manipulation which creates a false narrative that the victim then goes on to believe – for instance, believing that they are the cause of all problems in the friendship, when it is, in fact, the other party's fault) and social isolation or exclusion. Relational aggression is far more common among female–female friendships than male–male or female–male ones, hence the 'mean-girl' label.[5] More than two-thirds of teen girls state that they don't 'feel good enough' and this low self-esteem is often an underlying cause behind relational aggression in female friendships, in both the perpetrator and the victim.[6] If young people feel good about themselves, they are less likely to try to make others feel bad; similarly, if they feel good about themselves, they are less likely to internalise emotional aggression from others.

It can be heartbreaking if your young person finds themselves on the receiving end of relational aggression. Your job here is to bolster them and help them first to recognise and then escape the toxic relationship. This is definitely a time when you need to be the adult, listen more than you talk, try to lift your young person's spirits and provide them with unconditional support. Often, if a young person is on the receiving end of relational aggression, you will notice a change in their behaviour before you find out what is happening. They may be quieter and more withdrawn at home, or they may be snappier and more short-tempered than usual. They may also try to get out of going to school or college, or clubs and activities, especially if the perpetrator attends, too.

When your young person does open up to you, remember to ask them if they want advice or just want you to listen. If they just want you to listen, reassure them that they are wonderful and deserve friends who treat them well. If they want your advice, help them to see what is happening. Being mind-minded works well here, considering how the so-called friend is feeling and what may be spurring them on to behave in such a toxic way. This isn't an excuse for their behaviour, but when your young person understands that their friend is probably behaving in an unpleasant way because they are feeling bad, it helps them to not take the behaviour so personally. It's incredibly unlikely that their so-called friend's behaviour will change, so these sorts of scenarios usually end with your young person realising that they deserve more and ending the friendship. Anybody who gossips about them, excludes them or manipulates them is not a true friend. Ultimately, your young person needs to be encouraged to make new friends – ones who will support and cherish them – however, it's better if you help them to come to this conclusion themselves, rather than trying to dictate who they should or should not be friends with.

Moving on

Some friendships break down through no fault of either party, instead coming to a natural conclusion. This is particularly common during times of educational transition, for instance starting high school, the beginning of sixth form or college, or leaving to start work or the transition to university. If this happens to your young person, reassure them that a shift in friendships is normal – it is most likely nothing they've done wrong, but some friendships just come to an end as the individuals involved naturally change and grow. While your young person may have been close with their best friend from eleven to eighteen, they may find themselves drifting apart as their lives begin to take different directions. There is no dramatic falling-out, no relational or physical aggression, no break-up, just prolonged silence and a realisation that they have become very different people from who they were a year or two before.

My own teen best friend and I drifted apart in this way. We

never fell out. I went to university, she started work, and con-tact between us lessened to the point that we hadn't spoken for a couple of years. We briefly reconnected when our firstborns arrived, before drifting again for a decade, and then, after one final attempt at reconnecting, it became apparent that while we still cared for each other and enjoyed many wonderful memo-ries together, the past alone wasn't a strong enough reason to continue the friendship into the present. It wasn't sad. I remain grateful for the friendship we shared in adolescence and prefer to hold on to those precious memories over any stilted and awk-ward conversations we may try to have in the present if we were to keep trying to revive a dying friendship. Some friendships are not meant to be for life, but merely a season. Helping your young person to realise this and know when to gracefully let go is a gift to them.

Sibling relationships

While we would dearly love our young people to have perfect re-lationships with their siblings, in reality sibling relationships are complicated. It is not uncommon to find teenage siblings who constantly bicker and insult each other. As parents we naturally find these fraught relationships hard to handle and often feel the need to dive in and try to restore peace as soon as possible. If you speak with adults in their forties, fifties and older who have siblings and ask them what their relationship was like with them during their teen years, most often they will say 'Oh, we fought like mad, but we get on great now!'

Please don't worry if your teenage siblings don't seem to like each other at the moment, I'm almost certain the animosity won't last. Take the pressure off them and instead of trying to force friendship, accept that treating each other with respect is all that is needed right now. The friendship will happen naturally in the years to come. There is a positive to sibling bickering, too. If our teens have the opportunity to practise resolving arguments and having heated debates with their siblings, they are more likely to develop valuable, mature, interpersonal skills as they enter their twenties and beyond.

Romantic relationships

A social media poll of 2,000 adults, reported on by the *Independent*, focusing on the age at which most common life events occur, found that most young people will have their first romantic relationship at around the age of fifteen and most will have had their first serious relationship by seventeen, followed closely by their first heartbreak once they turn eighteen.[7] Romantic relationships in adolescence are an important part of development, impacting a young person's identity and laying the groundwork for all future relationships. Research has shown that young people in their teens who have positive romantic relationships are more likely to have positive ones in adulthood.[8] Dating helps them to understand others, increases empathy and improves social skills that positively affect all relationships they have, not just romantic ones.

Chatting with your young person about the signs of a positive relationship is crucial if they have already begun dating. If they haven't, it's still an important conversation to have, obviously with no pressure on them to try to find a partner.

What makes a good relationship?

- Mutual respect
- Mutual trust
- Honesty
- Kindness to each other
- Open communication

- Understanding and empathy for each other
- Healthy boundaries
- Supporting each other's goals and ambitions
- Retaining individual hobbies and friends
- Both partners feeling equal in the relationship
- Consent

Perhaps most importantly, encourage your young person to trust their instincts. If something doesn't feel quite right, then it probably isn't. If they are unhappy in a relationship, they shouldn't stay in it out of fear of upsetting the other person.

While healthy romantic relationships can impact a young person's development positively, toxic ones can have lasting negative effects on their mental health.[9] Far too many young people are unaware of red flags in a romantic relationship, and coercion and domestic abuse (physical or emotional) can – and do – start in adolescence. If your young person is dating, it's so important to discuss these red flags, not just with an emphasis on them being on the receiving end of them, but also perhaps unconsciously being the perpetrator.

The following are common relationship red flags:

- One person having all the control and making all the decisions
- Monitoring the actions and movement of the other partner (for example, tracking their social media logins and locations)
- Overdependence on each other
- Losing individual identity, interests and hobbies
- Lying
- Not trusting each other
- Humiliation or embarrassment caused by the partner
- Feeling as if they have to walk on eggshells around their partner for fear of upsetting them

- Jealousy
- Isolation from family or friends
- Any form of physical violence, even if it only happens once
- Lack of respect for boundaries or consent
- Manipulation
- Gaslighting, where one partner is made to feel that any problems are their fault

If your young person does identify any red flags and comes to you for support, remember 'two ears, one mouth': ask if they'd like you just to listen or to provide advice. Resist any temptation to say, 'I told you so!' or, 'I never liked them'. You don't want to undermine your young person, make them feel guilty for the relationship or reduce the chances of them coming to you for help and support in the future.

Talking about sex and consent

A study of over 11,000 young people provides us with an insight into the age at which young people engage in light, medium and heavy sexual-related activities.[10] Light activities were deemed as handholding and kissing, medium were classified as touching and fondling under clothing, and heavy was used to define oral sex and sexual intercourse. The results found that at fourteen years of age, 58 per cent had engaged in 'light' activities, 7.5 per cent had engaged in 'medium' activities and just over 3 per cent had engaged in 'heavy' activities. These figures are significantly lower than those from previous generations. Of those born during the 1980s, 30 per cent had had sex before they were sixteen years old and 20 per cent before they were fifteen.

Although it may be deeply uncomfortable to think about your young person being sexually active, it is something that is going to happen, if it hasn't already. You have two choices here: either you can bury your head in the sand or you can be the adult and work on why you feel so uncomfortable. If you want your young person to understand consent, use contraception, avoid an accidental pregnancy or sexually transmitted infection (STI) and have a positive relationship with sex, then you simply cannot choose option one. The more open you are with your young person and the more able they feel to talk to you about their worries, the more chance you will have of keeping them safe. Ignoring the issue or telling them to be abstinent won't work and could put them in danger.

What should you discuss with your young person, then? Let's cover a few of the most important points.

Consent

All young people should understand what it means when some-body says 'no' or 'stop', even if they say it during a sexual act. They should know that consent can be rescinded at any time and should be respected. Young people need to know that they should always be able to say 'no', even within a loving and com-mitted relationship, and it is always better to get their partner's consent before doing anything. Talk about how drinking alcohol or taking drugs (again, telling them not to do these things won't stop them – focusing on reducing risk is much more effective at keeping them safe) can impact a person's ability to make deci-sions and give consent. Finally, make sure they understand the legalities around consent. In the UK, the age of consent for any sexual activity is sixteen. However, it is illegal for somebody over the age of eighteen to engage in sexual activity with somebody under eighteen if they are in a position of authority or trust (a teacher, for instance, or they run a sporting class that the young person attends). In the USA, the age of consent varies by state: in most it is sixteen, however in some it is seventeen (for instance, in Colorado and Texas) or eighteen (for instance, in California and Florida).

Contraception and STIs

If your young person is straight, bisexual or pansexual (being attracted to a person and their soul, regardless of their sex or gender), you need to talk about the risks of pregnancy, as well as STIs and how to prevent them. If your young person is gay, or you don't know their sexual orientation, then talking about STI prevention is still important. If you have a daughter, explain that once they feel they may want to be sexually active, you would be happy to go to the doctor or family-planning clinic with them if they would like to consider long-acting reversible contraception (LARC), such as an implant. This is the contraception of choice for about 25 per cent of young people.[11] Over 60 per cent of young people prefer to use condoms purchased from retail shops as their choice of contraception, although this may be because they are not aware of other, longer-lasting alternatives. Demystifying contraception as soon as possible is the key to making these sorts of conversations feel less awkward and ensuring your young person is protected when they become sexually active.

Unplanned pregnancies

The rate of unplanned pregnancies in young people under the age of eighteen has more than halved in the last decade, now standing at 13 conceptions out of 1,000 girls down from 30 in 1,000 in 2011.[12] If your young person, or their partner, suspects they are pregnant, the only respectful way for you to respond is to support them. They need to make decisions about their future without coercion or control from you. What you may prefer that they do may not align with what they want to do, but pushing your beliefs could cause severe stress and trauma, which could permanently damage your relationship with them. If they feel they cannot continue with the pregnancy, they may make risky decisions that could endanger their health if you are not there for them. Make clear to your young person that you will support them, no matter what they choose to do, and seek professional guidance to help them decide and research the next steps. Remember, your hopes and dreams for their future are exactly that – *your* hopes and dreams – and they may not coincide with your young person's current thoughts.

Should you allow your young person's partner to stay in their room?

I'm going to answer this by asking you a different question: would you prefer your young person to have sex with their partner in a car, parked in a public place where they may be observed or caught by the police, or in the privacy and safety of their bedroom? As much as we may try to prohibit young people from engaging in sexual activities in their own homes, this is not a realistic approach. To put it bluntly, if they want to have sex, they will. And if it doesn't happen in your home, it *will* happen elsewhere. So while you may not feel comfortable with the idea of it happening under your own roof, it's better than receiving a call from the police station when they've been cautioned or charged with 'outraging public decency', and a lot cheaper for your young person than booking into a hotel.

It's a good idea to have some boundaries in place at home, such as encouraging all family members to knock on closed doors before entering, being aware of noise and respecting quiet times at night. You may also want to have boundaries in place concerning the length of time your young person and their partner have been together before they are allowed to stay the night. But these are all personal decisions for you to make to-gether as a family, and as difficult as the conversations may feel, they must be had.

Getting on with your young person's new partner

If you suspect that your young person has a new partner, allow them to break the news to you in their own time. Similarly, don't rush them to bring them home so that you can meet them. I'm sure you remember how awkward it felt when you brought your first boyfriend or girlfriend home, so it doesn't take too much to imagine how your young person feels. When you do meet them, hold back on the teasing, and embarrassing questions, and resist the temptation to bring out the naked-baby photos.

If you don't like their new partner, the best thing you can do is to keep your opinion to yourself (the only caveat here being if you notice any red flags of toxic behaviour, as mentioned on p. 169). If you try to encourage your young person to break up with their partner, it will only backfire and, you never know, this person may be the one they want to spend the rest of their life with. The best thing you can do is to be welcoming and respectful and try to get to know the partner. Maybe they will be a short-term thing or maybe this will be your new son- or daughter-in-law. Whichever way things go, it's never wrong to be kind.

Pornography

One way that growing up online has affected the relationships of young people is the ease with which they are able to access pornography (porn). Gone are the days of a group of teenagers shuffling into a newsagent and trying to buy a magazine from the top shelf; now our young people have the whole adult entertainment industry at their fingertips. In 2022, a survey of thirteen- to seventeen-year-olds revealed that 73 per cent of those asked said they had watched online porn at least once.[13] Of those, over half reported that they had viewed it by the time they were only thirteen. While a third of the young people surveyed said they had come across pornographic material by accident, 44 per cent said they had deliberately sought it out and, of these, over 70 per cent said they had watched porn within the last week.

While we may believe that our young people wouldn't watch porn, the statistics are sobering. And you can't rely only on parental controls on your young person's devices because pretty much every young person knows how to circumvent these with VPNs or similar. You have to sit down and talk with your young person about porn. They need to understand why it is problematic, how many involved in the industry are exploited, how it can become an unhealthy addiction and, most importantly, how it does not portray realistic, loving sexual relationships.

Sending and receiving sexually explicit imagery

Sexting and sharing explicit imagery is not unusual among young people. Research has revealed that almost 10 per cent of high-school students (aged between eleven and eighteen) admit to having sent sexually explicit images of themselves to others, while almost 40 per cent say they have received similar from others.[14]

In the last couple of years there has been more than one incident local to me where explicit photos of students have been circulated around the school population, which is not only exceptionally distressing for the young person in the images, but also illegal, because of the possession of indecent images of a minor. It is crucial that young people know that while they believe images may be private, they can be shared with others and kept long after they have separated from their partner. These images can be used for blackmail or just to humiliate the original sender. Even sending via time-limited messaging services, such as Snapchat, is not safe because the images can be screenshot and shared or stored.

If your young person is on the receiving end of unwanted explicit imagery, discuss with them actions they can take – for instance, reporting to their school or the social media service provider the message was received on. Explain that it is better for them to delete and block than respond, as many people 'get off' on the responses (there is a specific sexual quirk where individuals enjoy being humiliated and shamed). Most importantly, reiterate to your young person that if they receive images or messages which make them feel uncomfortable, they can always talk to you or another trusted adult about anything and ask for your help at any time.

MISOGYNY, INFLUENCERS AND PODCASTERS

There is a rising trend of influencers and podcasters with huge reaches who are becoming rich and famous, and who possess misogynistic views. Often, and perhaps more dangerously, they speak about general issues and have opinions which seem sound around 80 to 90 per cent of the time. These views quickly go viral and their content is shared, often among teen boys, raising the profile of the individual. Their remaining content, littered with disgusting misogyny, as well as racism and homophobia, then garners huge amounts of attention.

These influencers and podcasters draw huge audiences

of young males, who quickly start to absorb their views on how girls should be treated. One such is British–American kick-boxer Andrew Tate, who stated in 2017: 'Females are the ultimate status symbol amongst elite players. I go out and f*ck and I come back to her and I don't care about her and I only love my girl. That's not cheating, that's exercise.'[15] These messages are heard by hundreds of thousands of male young people, who start to believe that this is how girls should be treated. As parents and carers, it is our duty to correct this and teach our young people (especially if we have sons) to respect each other.

Supporting your LGBTQ+ child

Just under 7 per cent of young people in the UK identify as LGBTQ+ (lesbian, gay, bisexual, transgender, queer and other identities), which is roughly double the figure for those over twenty-one.[16] Young people today are a lot more open about their sexuality than those from previous generations, but that doesn't necessarily mean that your young person has felt able to open up to you yet, or even worked things out themselves. You may have an inkling, but don't try to force your young person to come out to you if they haven't done so already. Similarly, don't presume you know how they identify or try to label their sexuality for them. It really is paramount that you allow your young person to decide who they are and how they want to tell you in their own time. Most importantly, your young person needs to know that you love them unconditionally and that this is unwavering, whoever they love.

Make sure that if you talk about future partners, you don't make assumptions. For instance, instead of saying, 'When you have a wife/husband', say, 'When you make a life with the person you love'. Similarly, if other family members or friends make comments that are homophobic, be sure to pick them up on them and correct their disrespectful comments. Knowing that you are an ally and a safe place is crucial for your young person, especially if they face adversity from the outside world.

What if your young person isn't interested in dating?

Two-thirds of thirteen- to seventeen-year-olds have never dated.[17] Young people today are waiting longer to begin relationships than those in previous generations – maybe because they are more interested in their hobbies or their studies, or maybe they haven't found 'the one' yet. Some, however, identify as asexual (often abbreviated to 'ace'). Young people may find themselves attracted to somebody emotionally, and even physically, but have no interest in sexual activity with them. A poll of young people who identify as LGBTQ+ found that 10 per cent identify as asexual (or somewhere on the ace spectrum – a spectrum relating to different types and levels of asexuality).[18] If your young person doesn't seem interested in dating, don't push them for information about who they may like or pry about their sexual feelings. Instead, allow them to open up in their own time.

Helping with heartbreak

It is inevitable that your young person will have to deal with heartbreak at some point in their life, and the chances of it happening during their teens or early twenties is high. When it does happen, take them seriously. Don't be tempted to downplay their feelings or the enormity of what has happened in their world. It may be tempting to say something like, 'Don't worry, there are plenty more fish in the sea', but to your young person this just says that you don't understand them. While we, as adults, know it is more than likely that in a few months they will have moved on and be happy with a new partner, losing somebody they believed they loved feels like the end of the world to a young person. What they need when this happens is for us to listen more than we talk, along with the offer of hugs, hot cups of tea, comforting blankets, a freshly baked cake and a soppy movie. The heartbreak will heal, but it won't go away any quicker if we belittle it, and if we do that we run the risk of our young people not feeling able to come to us with their romantic concerns in the future.

Young people and parasocial relationships

One type of relationship we haven't yet mentioned in this chapter, but that is common among young people, is the parasocial relationship. These are one-sided relationships – for instance, those with a social media influencer or pop star, where the young person believes that they know the individual well. Commonly, young people will talk about a celebrity as if they are friends, invested in their thoughts, feelings and activities. Sometimes they will discuss social media influencers and refer to them as their friends. I think most of us can think back to our teens and remember a crush on a pop star, sports personality or actor. Sometimes we would have fantasies about meeting them, or even dating them. Perhaps we had impressive knowledge of their lives, adorning our bedrooms with pictures of them. As we grew up, for most of us the connection would lessen, since parasocial relationships are most common during adolescence, however they do still exist for some in adulthood. Research has shown that over 60 per cent of young people have some sort of parasocial relationship that leads them to think they have a connection with a favourite celebrity or influencer.[19]

Parasocial relationships even have nicknames, depending upon the celebrity and their 'stans' or fandoms, including: Swifties, Harries, Beliebers, Arianators and BeyHive (you can probably guess who each one refers to). Male young people are most likely to feel a connection to sports stars, while females are more likely to feel it with actors, particularly emotional, platonic connections with female actors.[20]

These types of relationships are an important part of a young person's identity development, helping them to decide who they want to be and who they want to spend time with. They can also help those who are struggling with feelings of loneliness or social exclusion and can trigger the forming of new friendships among those in shared fandoms. Instead of trying to stop them or talk your young person out of them, they should be seen as a normal part of adolescence and perfectly healthy, so long as the young person does not place these relationships above real ones, causing them to increasingly isolate themselves from others. If you are ever worried that your young person's parasocial relationships are negatively affecting their everyday life, speak to your family doctor or call a specialist adolescent mental-health charity's helpline (see Resources, p. 235).

I hope this chapter has helped to answer some questions you may have had about your young person's relationships of whatever kind. Navigating any type of relationship during adolescence can be a tricky time and, unsurprisingly, our young people need our support, especially when things aren't going well or to plan. Building trust with them and letting them know that they can talk to us about anything with as little judgement as possible from us is the key to helping them form happy, healthy relationships, both now and in the future.

Chapter 9

Increasing Independence

To raise a child, who is comfortable enough to leave you, means you've done your job. They are not ours to keep, but to teach them to soar on their own.

Author unknown

Society often places young people as the butt of jokes, laughing about how useless they are, incapable of doing anything for themselves. Whole TV programmes and even feature films have become popular based on this very idea. While we may chuckle at these jokes and shows, and many of the plot lines may ring true for us as parents and carers of young people, there is an underlying issue that needs to be addressed: if our young people are so ill-equipped for 'the real world', as many would say, then who is to blame? If young people don't even know that they don't know how to do something, then we cannot blame them. The blame has to lie squarely at our feet, for failing to teach them. The irony that it is grown adults, usually parents and carers, laughing at these jokes is not lost on me – because what they are really laughing at is the fact that they haven't done a great job preparing their young people for independent life.

Of course, even we, as adults, aren't aware of everything we should prepare our young people for. It recently came to my attention that my twenty-year-old had no idea how to buy postage stamps or even address an envelope, despite the fact that at the time he had a temporary job as a delivery driver for Royal Mail. Very often, we only realise that our young people don't know how to do something when disaster strikes – for example, they shrink an expensive item of clothing or dye it bright red in the wash. Then it dawns on us that perhaps we should have taken the time to teach them how to do laundry.

My aim with this chapter is to help you and your young person work towards independence, preparing them for a life away from you, whether that is in a few months' or a decade's time.

What should young people know?

You've already taught your young person a lot, but now you need to teach them to do all the little things that you've always done for them, especially those that they didn't notice or took for granted. So what should young people know by the time they reach adulthood?

- How to do laundry – including separating whites and coloureds, how to hand wash, how to hang washing to dry, how to iron and how to get something dry cleaned
- How to do grocery shopping – including how to meal prep and write a shopping list, how to select foods based on freshness and price, and how to understand supermarket offers and deals, especially when they're not as good value as they might seem at first
- How to safely prepare and store food (more on this later in this chapter)
- How to do housework – including how to dust and

hoover, clean a bathroom, clean an oven and wash
a floor

- How to empty a rubbish bin and put bins out for
collection
- How to sew on a button or patch and repair simple rips
on clothing
- How to make a medical or dental appointment and
understand how prescription charges work
- How to dose painkillers (including paracetamol and
NSAIDs such as aspirin and ibuprofen)
- How to cope with a medical emergency (including how
to stop bleeding, clean and dress a wound, CPR, and
when to attend accident and emergency)
- How to plan a journey on public transport (including
navigating timetables, ticket purchases and maps – of
the London Underground, for example)
- How to send a letter or parcel to somebody (including
packaging, weighing, ordering a courier or taking to
the post office)
- How to manage personal finances (more on this later
in this chapter)
- How to pay tax (including registering as self-employed,
understanding pay slips and deductions)
- How to use a debit and credit card, and the difference
between them
- How to apply for and manage a loan and mortgage
(and an understanding of interest)
- How to apply for and manage a private rental
property – including the difference between different
types of tenancies
- How to write a CV, search for and apply for jobs, and
sit an interview (more on p. 200)
- How to do basic maintenance on a car, especially if
they drive or will shortly learn to do so – including

fuelling, changing a tyre, checking oil levels, topping
up screenwash and de-icing windows

This list is clearly not exhaustive and there may be many
more things that your young person will need to learn based
upon their own individual circumstances. I should also point out
that this is a list to aim towards by the time your young person
is twenty-one, not one where they should tick off every point,
especially not if your young person is younger, neurodiverse or
has any disabilities. This list is simply here to give you some idea
of what your young person may benefit from learning and also
to discuss with them, to find out what they want to learn. Your
list may look very different to mine and that's OK!

Helping your young person learn how to rectify a mistake

We've spoken lots about executive-function development and
how young people struggle in stressful situations. They will tend
to panic a lot more than adults when their best-laid plans don't
work out, or if something goes wrong unexpectedly. Whereas
most adults are able to think logically and rationally, working
through steps to resolve a difficult situation in their minds,
young people are likely to either stick their heads in the sand
and hope the issue goes away (a typical 'freeze' stress response)
or panic and try to distance themselves from it (a typical 'flight'
stress response). While you should obviously support your young
person through any difficult situations they find themselves in,
your ultimate aim is to provide the scaffolding so that they can
rectify tricky situations independently.

One of my young people, who had recently started university,
called me in a panic. He had gone to the nearby supermarket to
buy some toilet roll having run out (remembering young people

are not so good at hypothetical thinking, or planning for the future, therefore running out of various important items is not an uncommon occurrence for them), and when he returned to his shared flat he believed his flatmates were playing a prank on him as the living room had been rearranged. He was very confused as to why they would do such a thing. He also mentioned that his bedroom door key had stopped working and he was locked out of his room, despite hammering on the door several times trying to get it to open. He had, however, had the foresight to contact the building's reception and ask them to send a maintenance person to fix his door lock.

With my adult brain, and probably with yours, it was very quickly apparent that he was in the wrong flat. This thought hadn't entered his head, however. Once I had explained my reasoning to him, his panic ramped up a gear as he realised he was trespassing, and so he quickly ran out of the flat, leaving his newly purchased toilet roll outside somebody else's bedroom. Once he was safely back in his own flat, however, his anxiety worsened – he became worried about the maintenance person knocking on an unknown person's door and being caught out for trespassing. I had to encourage him to breathe and calm down, then suggested that he should go back to reception and explain the situation to them, cancelling the maintenance callout and apologising. Again, he had not thought of this in the heat of the moment. He reluctantly agreed but was worried about the response of the people working in reception. I reassured him he had nothing to worry about and asked him to report back to me after he had spoken to them. As you would imagine, he later reported back that the reception staff had just laughed when he had explained what had happened, much to his relief.

After some more calming down, I reminded him that he still didn't have any toilet roll – and since his building had more than twenty floors, each with five flats, it was unlikely that he would track down the one he had accidentally entered, so he would have to go to the supermarket again to buy more. The whole ordeal lasted for almost two hours from the original toilet-roll run to toilet-roll run number two. While it was clear to me that he needed to rectify the maintenance call-out and make reception aware of what had happened, as well as buying more toilet roll of course, my young person's brain had other ideas and sent him into a tailspin. Important lessons were learned that day and now he is more able to take a breath and work out steps to resolve any possible future problems he finds himself in. Of course, I didn't take the scaffolding away all at once, though. He knows he can call me if he ever struggles with something else in the future, but the panic calls have definitely lessened since what is now known in our family as 'toilet-roll-gate'.

Raising a financially literate young person

With the cost of living soaring, helping your young person to understand how to manage their finances and avoid getting into debt is more important than ever. We simply can't leave it up to schools to teach them everything they need to know.

Of course, we have already taught our young people lots about managing finances, unconsciously – every time we talk about money, look for discounts, try to save money or have conversations about cutting back, they are listening and they learn a great deal from the role modelling we provide. So if you're not the greatest role model here, it's even more important that you have frank and honest conversations with your young person about money, explaining that you know you may not have set the greatest example, but that you'd like to teach them how to be better, while trying to improve with money yourself, too.

What sort of things should you discuss with your young person?

- The difference between credit and debit cards, and understanding how interest rates work for credit cards
- How interest works, both on savings and borrowings, and knowing how to compare interest rates
- How overdrafts work and the difference between a planned and an unplanned one
- How savings work and the different types of savings accounts available to them
- The difference between child and adult bank accounts, and how to change or open their own or move to a student account if they are attending university
- How to save for a pension (it's never too early!)
- How to budget and fill in a monthly budget planner
- How to be aware of online scams and phishing emails and phone calls trying to steal their money
- How to shop around for a best buy, and how to save money by shopping preloved
- How to make extra money by selling unwanted items
- How cryptocurrency works and which forms and trading places are legitimate
- The difference between saving and investing

Young people should also understand how poverty affects families, how people end up in poverty, often through no fault for their own, how the benefits system works and which charities can help to support those who are struggling financially – if not for themselves, then simply to improve their empathy for others.

Teaching your young person how to cook

If you haven't already taught your young person how to cook some basic and nutritious meals, now is the time to do so. And if you are not the greatest cook yourself, this is the perfect chance for you to learn together.

Spending time in the kitchen with your young person is a great bonding opportunity (despite the mess, and typical young-person emotional behaviour) and you will be giving them skills that will significantly improve their lives as they branch out into becoming independent. If your young person plans to head to university or move into their own accommodation in the not-too-distant future, teaching them how to meal plan, shop for groceries, prepare food, cook, serve and store it will make their transition much smoother. This is also a lovely chance to pass on treasured family recipes, either by teaching your young person how to cook them, writing them down in a notebook or having a little bound book made, so they can hold on to them and even pass them down to their own children one day.

What should your young person know about cooking?

- How to read cooking instructions on store-bought food
- How to follow a recipe (including weighing ingredients)
- How to use an oven and a hob (and the difference between electric and gas settings)
- How to use air fryers, slow cookers and microwaves, if you have them
- The correct oven temperatures to use for different foods
- How to peel, chop, finely dice and julienne vegetables
- How to cook pasta and rice
- How to boil an egg, both soft and hard-boiled
- How to defrost food safely
- How to select fresh fruit and vegetables in stores
- Where to store fresh foods (for example in a dark cupboard or the fridge)
- Different baking techniques such as creaming and

folding (lest your young person should re-enact 'that' episode of *Schitt's Creek* – if you know, you know!)
- How long to store different items and the difference between 'Best before' and 'Use by'
- Basic kitchen hygiene
- How to cook on a low budget

If you can teach your young person to make at least five budget meals from scratch, you will make a huge difference to them when they leave home. Far too many young people live independently on diets of takeaways, frozen pizzas and ramen, which isn't good for their health or their bank balance.

Learning to drive

Your young person learning to drive is both an exciting and terrifying thought. I have never felt as anxious as a parent as I have when my young people started to drive, and especially when they passed their tests and started to drive alone. I remember thinking that the sleepless nights couldn't get worse than they were in babyhood and toddlerhood, then my young people started driving and I found myself lying in bed awake, anxiously awaiting the sound of their keys in the front-door lock before I could go to sleep. The only thing I can suggest here is that you learn to accept the anxiety and see it as a sign that you are a caring parent. Asking them to drop you a quick text when they have arrived somewhere safely can go a long way to allaying your fears; similarly, if they are going to be later home than expected, ask them to let you know, just so that you don't worry about them.

When it comes to learning to drive, there really isn't a wrong or a right way. Some young people and their parents or carers do well without professional driving lessons (I am absolutely not patient enough for this, but if you are then you have my full respect!), while others benefit very much from them. The pro of paying for driving lessons is undoubtedly the avoidance of arguments and stress when you take your young person out to drive and they almost crash your car. The downside is the cost. Driving lessons are prohibitively expensive, and simply unaffordable for many. If they are out of your reach, then suggesting that your young person get a part-time job to pay for them is a really good solution.

When your young person has passed their driving test and is ready to drive alone, it is vital that you discuss safety with them. We already learned in Chapter 2 that young people are more reckless drivers if they have passengers in the car with them, and it is important to talk to them about this. If they are going to have friends in their car, they have to be aware of the potential impact on their driving and adjust accordingly. Make sure they are aware of the effects of speeding – not just potential legal issues, but the impact of speeding on their own safety and that of others. Conversations about drinking and driving and drugs and driving should happen as soon as possible, even if your young person doesn't drink or take drugs – there is always a first time and they need to understand how their driving may be impacted, as well as the legalities.

Opting for a telematics (black-box) insurance policy is a great idea for new and inexperienced drivers. The 'box' tracks the speed young people drive at, as well as erratic braking, and most insurers issue a report each month, indicating problem areas and areas for improvement. These reports can provide a great basis for you to have ongoing chats about driving safety with your young person, and the policies are almost always significantly cheaper than non-box ones.

Make sure your young person knows what to do if they have an accident – that they must always stop and take the details of the other party, including their name, address, registration number and insurer's details, even if they don't believe there is any damage. Encourage them also to take photographs or, better still, fit a dashcam in the car they will be driving.

And finally, ensure they learn how to fill their car with petrol (if they have a petrol car) before their first solo drive. You would be amazed at the number of young people who have never learned how to operate a fuel pump and get caught out the first time they have to refuel their car alone (yes, I do speak from experience!).

All that said, not all young people are keen to drive as soon as they are legally able to. Some don't feel ready and others don't see the point just yet, which is fine. There is nothing to gain from pushing your young person into learning if they aren't ready for it – it will just cause unnecessary stress and tension for you all.

Planning for first holidays alone

While you may have enjoyed some lovely family holidays and breaks with your young person, there comes a time when they are going to want to spend time with their friends or partners and not you. It can be really hard not to take this personally and feel that your young person is somehow saying they don't want to spend time with you any more because they don't enjoy your company. But this is just part of them spreading their wings, so instead of feeling sad, or angry, celebrate that you've built a great attachment with your young person and that the gift of independence you have given them means they now feel safe to explore the world without that close proximity to you. You've done a great job and your young person's choice to spend their holidays away from you is testament to this.

If your young person is planning to go off on their first break or holiday, check that they have a solid, reliable plan in place and emergency backups. If they need help looking for travel providers, talk about ways they can assess a company's reliability, using Trustpilot reviews, for example, or ABTA and ATOL protection. Talk about the importance of travel insurance if they are travelling outside of their main country of residence and tips to keep themselves safe – for instance, in areas with a high incidence of pickpocketing or with regard to drinking-water supplies and mosquito protection. Help them to understand the process of checking in for flights and clearing security at an airport, emphasising that they should never take anything from strangers at airports, with role-playing at home if they are anxious or neurodivergent. Reiterate that they can contact you at any time if they are scared, anxious or confused about anything, or if they just miss home and want a chat.

Finally, try to relax – your young person going away without you for the first time is a big deal for both of you, and you are going to have some big feelings about it, but try to trust in them and in yourself and all the preparation you have put in that has allowed them to get to this point.

Future plans

Maybe your young person has already decided on a future career, or perhaps they are already at university, in an apprenticeship or at work. If they aren't sure what they want to do, however, chatting about career options, in addition to any provision at school or college, can be helpful. You should view these conversations as exploration, free of bias on your part. You may think they are well suited to a certain career or field of study, or you may hope that they will continue the family tradition of a specific job, but trying to steer, or indeed force, young people never works out. They have to choose what they want to do alone. Remember, it's not your future we're talking about here.

Remember too that your young person's identity is still a work in progress. They may simply not have any idea what they want to do in the future yet, and that's OK. Or maybe their long-held dream has faded and they want to switch to something entirely different. I've always thought it entirely ridiculous that young people with still-developing brains and identities are forced at only eighteen to choose how they want to spend the rest of their lives, especially considering that just a few months beforehand they couldn't even legally choose somebody to vote for. It's OK that your young person tries on many career hats for size until they find one that fits. This may include switching courses, apprenticeships, traineeships or leaving a good job they have previously worked in.

If your young person does well at school, you may be tempted to encourage them to pursue an academic path – A-levels, university and maybe postgraduate study – but not all young people are suited to this path, even if they are capable. Many will do much better in a job, especially in trades that require more practical or physical work. These are just as valuable as careers attained via a traditional college or university route and often pay better, without burdening young people with huge student loans. Or perhaps your young person will be happiest in an arts-based job, or something that utilises their computing, gaming or social media skills. Remember, what doesn't sound like 'a proper job' to us oldies can often be a highly lucrative and rewarding position for young people. Too often, parents and carers try to influence young people's career choices based on what was thought to be 'a good job' when they themselves were in their teens or early twenties, but life moves on. The jobs market is very different now from when we were young people.

Starting university

If it seems as if your young person is heading towards university, there are three main times when they will need your help and support: choosing a university, preparing to start and settling in once they've started. Let's break these down, one by one.

Choosing a university

So your young person thinks they may want to go to university. What can you do to help them? If they're still in the selecting and application process, the most important thing you can do is to let them choose. Once again, it's not about where you want them to go. I know I've banged on and on about this, but it really is unbelievably important. Your young person will be studying and most importantly living at the university (or close to it) for at least three years, so they need to choose somewhere they will feel both comfortable and inspired to live and study.

Encourage them to look at the university websites and social media pages and take part in online open-day tours, combined with checking entry requirements for each course to make a short list of some that they would like to visit in person. This list should absolutely not revolve around the choices of their friends, unless that happens coincidentally. If you don't have transport, or the cost of fuel is prohibitive, some universities offer a travel bursary scheme, where they will refund the cost of travel, or fuel, so that your young person is able to visit. Or perhaps they have friends attending open days and they can car pool. Once at the open day, if you go with them, try to rein in any enthusiasm or distaste and focus on your young person's feelings and opinions, so they can make their own informed choice of where to apply to. It's very likely they will have different views to you of what is and isn't important.

Once your young person gets their offers (and probably a rejection or two) and then their exam results, it's time for them to make a final decision about where they will study. If they get their first-choice place, then all is well, and it's time to celebrate; if not (and clearing – the process of getting a university place after results are out – isn't for them), or they are not sure if they are ready to start university just yet, then perhaps they will want to consider a gap year. This would allow them to work and save, trying on a few different career hats, travel or take time to resit exams to try to nudge their grades up a little. Gap years are a great idea for young people, but they are rarely taken.

Preparing to start university

The time from confirmation of securing a university place to your young person actually starting goes incredibly quickly. It's usually only a month or less, so it doesn't allow much time for preparation. For this reason, slowly encouraging your young person to prepare in the months running up to September can mean they feel better equipped.

What should your young person know before starting university? Pretty much everything we've covered so far in this chapter. In addition, when you know where they are going, taking a few day or weekend trips there, so they can settle into the area and learn where the supermarkets, station, bus stops, doctors, dentists, hospital and other important places are, can really help to take the edge off any anxiety when they start. As soon as your young person knows where they will be living, encourage them to search on social media for residents' chat groups to see if they can get to know their new flatmates or neighbours virtually, which makes moving-in day a little less daunting.

Finally, try to gather items that they will need to take with them a few months in advance. This helps to spread the cost and also means you will be able to watch out for sale bargains or people selling or giving away items on local selling sites. The following are the essentials for most new university students:

- Sheets, duvet and cover, pillows, pillowcases and mattress protector – usually for a 'small double' (4ft) bed
- Wastepaper bin
- Desk lamp
- Clothes hangers
- Two sets of bath and hand towels (one set to use while the other is washed)
- Bath mat
- Toilet brush and cleaning cloths if they have an en suite (they will need to clean it themselves)
- An old-fashioned alarm clock (the type they can't sleep through – mobiles are not enough!)
- At least two dinner plates, side plates and bowls (one for your young person, one for a guest)
- At least two glasses and mugs
- At least two place settings of cutlery
- Saucepan and frying pan
- Cooking utensils (for example, wooden spoon, spatula and fish slice)
- Tin opener
- Baking trays
- Chopping board
- Kitchen knife and scissors
- Tea towels
- Oven gloves
- Washing-up brush
- Posters/photos, to personalise room
- Cushions, to make things cosy
- Reminders of home

Some accommodations will come with a microwave and toaster, but many won't, so it's worth checking in advance, especially since a lot of young people tend to live on toast and microwave meals at university.

Settling in

On moving-in day, try to rein in your own emotions. You may be feeling sad at the loss of your 'baby', but they need you to be strong, so hold any tears in for the drive home, if you can. Don't badger your young person to contact you with updates constantly – it can put a lot of pressure on them when they're busy trying to socialise and meet new people, and if they haven't yet made friends, they may feel scared to tell you for fear of making you worry about them. A quick little text saying, 'Love you!' at bedtime is a good idea, so is a quick 'Hope things are going well' now and again. But hold back on the constant questions. All my young people have really appreciated being sent little notes and small gifts (like a packet of sweets) in the post, especially when they were feeling a bit down. The text notification most are sent by their accommodation provider saying, 'You have mail, come and collect it!' is a lovely surprise for them.

What should you do if your young person is struggling with settling in and you're worried about their mental health?

First off, help them to realise that most other students are feeling the same. It can take several months to feel settled in and once the fun of freshers' week is over, the proper work begins and inevitably 'freshers' flu' hits (a cold virus that spreads virulently among young people living in close proximity, just as it did at the start of each term when your young person was at nursery and infant school), leaving young people feeling a bit flat. Make sure your young person has details of people and places they can contact if they're feeling down and either don't want to or can't talk to you – for instance, in the middle of the night (see Resources, p. 235). If you are feeling particularly worried about them, encourage them to come home for a break or go to visit them if you can. Many universities have a number for student services which parents and carers can call if they feel their young person needs checking up on, so don't be afraid to contact them too if you are worried.

What if they want to drop out?

It's common for young people to consider dropping out of university, especially during the first semester. If your young person mentions that they are thinking about leaving, encourage them to chat with their personal tutor and student support. Sometimes swapping on to a different course will make them feel much happier, and the earlier they swap, the better.

If your young person is serious about wanting to drop out – many just feel that university is not for them after a while – then the best thing to do is to support them. I know of several students who dropped out of their courses but didn't tell their parents until the end of the academic year because they were worried about their reaction. The stress this causes is terrible for their mental health. One of my young people dropped out of his course halfway through, which was hard to take after he'd got so far, but he wasn't happy. We agreed he could come back home with a couple of boundaries: if his accommodation couldn't be re-let to another student, then he would have to work to pay the rent for the remainder of the year; we also agreed that he would come home and find a temporary job, while he looked for permanent positions, rather than having no future plans at all. Within two weeks of coming home he had found a good job and has never looked back. The experience may, at face value, seem a waste of time and money. However, the eighteen months he was away taught him how to live independently and his social skills were developed by learning to live with others and socialising with people of different ages and nationalities. The time away also helped him to decide what career he wanted to pursue and to become a more rounded person.

Starting work

If your young person is keen to start work, begin by investigating the different options open to them. For instance, they could consider an entry-level position, an internship, a volunteer position or temporary contract to gain experience, a traineeship or an apprenticeship.

In the UK, if your young person is under eighteen, they will need to opt for an apprenticeship or traineeship, unless they are also attending school or college. Apprenticeships are a great way for them to gain experience and qualifications, as well as earn a wage, and they are available in many different industries (for details of how to find one, see Resources, p. 235).

If your young person is struggling to choose a career, there are many free online career quizzes they can take. Reiterate, though, that they don't have to settle on a career now; gaining lots of experience in varied roles may be the best way to help them to decide what they ultimately want to do.

Another avenue to consider is that of your young person becoming self-employed. This is a route that is never covered during school career-education sessions, but it is a valid option, with around 10–20 per cent of the global population working for themselves. If your young person has a good idea and the passion to start their own business, then this may be the best option for them. As somebody who has been self-employed since I was in my mid-twenties, I cannot imagine ever working for anybody else again. There are downsides, of course, and it doesn't suit everybody, but the freedom it can bring is wonderful. One of my young people has been self-employed since the age of fifteen (there is no minimum age requirement) and has impressive turn-overs. Why entrepreneurship isn't covered more at school and promoted as a valid career option, I'll never understand.

Finding and applying for a job

If your young person decides they would like to apply for a job and doesn't know where to start, you can help by guiding them towards online careers websites, employment agencies and local adverts. I've spoken with a few young people who aren't working or in education about why they are not looking for a job, and far from the 'they're-just-being-lazy' answer many adults would give, they tell me they just don't know where to start. They don't know how to look for a job or apply for one, so they do nothing.

Helping your young person to write a CV and cover letter should be next on your list, followed by practising interview techniques. Again, don't just assume that your young person knows how to answer interview questions – many don't. Role-playing common ones can help prepare your young person to tackle difficult questions, avoid giving problematic responses and enable them to feel more confident and more likely to be successful at interview.

Should you charge your young person rent and board?

I volunteer for the charity Citizens Advice one day each week, and often speak to parents and carers who are struggling to make ends meet. I cannot tell you how many of them have grown-up children living with them – some into their mid- or late thir-ties – either working or in receipt of benefits but paying nothing towards the upkeep of the house, bills or food, let alone paying rent. When I propose that they ask their adult children to pay rent they often reply, 'But how can I broach the subject with them?' My suggestion to you is to have the discussion as soon as possible. You don't need to wait until your young person is working. If young people know that they will one day need to pay you rent, then it doesn't come as a shock to them, nor will you need to have an awkward conversation in the future.

What should you charge?

A common suggestion is using 20–25 per cent of their monthly income to set their rent payment. And rather than increasing each time they earn more (for instance, a bonus), keep the rate set for an agreed period of time. You should also discuss what exactly this payment will cover – say, lodging, breakfast, lunch and dinner, and gas, electricity and water, with any snacks, clothing, toiletries, phone bills, car expenses, entertainment and personal care (for example, hairdressing) being covered by them. What you do with the money is up to you and your personal financial situation. Some families will need to use it all to pay bills, while others may be able to keep some – or even all – of it in a secret savings account, so that when the young person moves out they have a little nest egg to cover a mortgage or rent deposit and perhaps something left over to go towards buying some furniture.

When should you start charging rent?

Again, that's up to you and your situation. I charge my young people rent from the time that they have their first full-time job. While they are at school, college or university they keep anything they earn from their part-time jobs. Having these boundaries set as soon as possible is key, though.

As young people edge ever closer to independence, our role as parents and carers is to ensure they are equipped with the tools

202 • How to Raise a Teen

they need to venture into life alone, alongside being ready and willing to offer our support whenever necessary. I spoke about the idea of scaffolding earlier in this book (see p. 184); now is the time to start to remove small parts of scaffolding that are no longer needed, little by little, without affecting the safety and security of the main supporting structure.

I often feel that this stage in parenting is a little like a game of Jenga, as you carefully test which bricks you can remove and which are still needed. Sometimes you try to take a block away, but it becomes apparent that your young person is not quite ready and the structure becomes unstable, so you quickly reinsert it and restart the backup support. There is never a time in parenting when your young person won't need you in some way, and your goal isn't to make yourself redundant, but to allow them to slowly become autonomous in a way that boosts their confidence and prepares them to launch themselves to fly when they are ready.

When they do take flight and you are left with the much-discussed 'empty nest', then what is next for you? That's exactly what we'll cover in the coming chapter.

Chapter 10

Letting Go

A mother's job is to teach her children not to need her anymore. The hardest part of that job is accepting success.

Rochelle B. Weinstein, American author

This quote has always resonated with me, but I don't think it is entirely true. Our young people will always need us in some way – that connection is never truly severed. I'm in my late forties and orphaned, but a week rarely passes when I don't wish my parents were still around and that I could call and discuss something with them. The beauty of working so hard in the 'holding-on' stage that we started this book with is that when you 'let go' the invisible string between you and your young person still exists. You feel pride at their accomplishments and growing independence; indeed, watching your once-stroppy teens growing into amazing young men and women is a wonderful reward for your patience.

This transition is bittersweet, though. As exciting as the future is, there are always moments when you miss the past a little. And the bigger your young people become, the more it drives home the message that their childhoods are gone, and that brings with it a strange sense of mourning. Our memories are often rose-tinted, and the saying 'The days are long, but the years are short' couldn't be truer. How quickly we forget the bone-crunching exhaustion of the early days of parenting, looking back wistfully at photos and videos of our now young people as chubby-faced, happy toddlers. While days in the early months and years may have felt impossibly long, the years ramped by like a horse's gallop. Sometimes it feels as if you can barely catch your breath, and every so often, you turn to see your young person, with their angular adult face, and are shocked at not seeing your little boy or girl as they once were.

So we have now come full circle, to the idea of letting go. This chapter is not for your young person, however. It's not about them or their behaviour. It's about you. For the last nine chapters we have been talking about preparing your young person, but now, as we come to the end, the focus needs to be on preparing you. While our young people face huge transitions during adolescence, they aren't the only ones. Parents and carers have to adapt to change, too, and your transition is no less important or huge than the one your young person is going through.

'The lasts'

Have you ever thought about the last time you did something with your young person?

When they are little, we commemorate their firsts: first steps, first words, first solid food, their first pair of shoes and the first time they sleep through the night. We take photos to stick in albums and share their pictures proudly on our social media. We call family and friends and let them know how exciting their new achievements are. Their lasts, however, either pass us by unconsciously, or we mark them with sorrow and regretful retrospect: the last school assembly or play, the last time we took them to a school disco, the last time we tucked them into bed at night, the last time we bought a toy.

The last Christmas toy purchase always gets me the most. You may be wondering why? Especially since it is surely the most materialistic of memories. But it marks such a strong line between childhood and approaching adulthood. Gone are the Christmases of the past where you would be handed a crumpled Christmas list with excitement, after they walked past the latest toy in a shop window with wide-eyed wonder. There are no more Christmas Eve nights spent trying to quietly assemble large toys, before draping them in wrapping paper, ready for eyes twinkling as brightly as fairy lights, and eager hands to rip into on Christmas morning. There are no more sounds of electric trains, toy police-car sirens or meowing electronic pet cats competing for attention over Christmas cartoons on TV. Now Christmas is silent. Christmas Eve is increasingly spent alone, waiting up for your young person to safely return from an evening out with their friends, and the morning is also quiet, as you wonder what time they will wake up and finally get out of bed to begin the festivities. The afternoons are often spent with their faces in a book or a screen, with headphones on. The silence of adolescence and early adulthood can be deafening. Never did you image you would miss the cacophony of early childhood, and yet here you are.

What can you do if you recognise these feelings? Honestly, I have no expert answers. You gradually become acclimatised to the new stage in your life. It makes you appreciate the little things more and cherish glimpses of how things used to be. If your young person asks you to play a board game with them or join them for a game on their new console, you accept without hesitation. You create new traditions, too. In my family, our crazy Christmas Eve nights have been replaced by a family Indian takeaway. It may sound a little dull, but it has become a beloved tradition that my young people never want to miss.

Each year, there is another seat at the table added, as their new partners join us and our family expands. I hope someday in the future even more chairs will be added as grandchildren are born, and so we will start the cycle of noise, flashing lights, ridiculously early morning wake-ups and discarded wrapping paper again. This time, however, I know I will appreciate it far more than I ever did before and can hopefully give my adult children a much-needed break as I take off their hands some of the night wakes, early mornings and constant requests to play.

They say youth is wasted on the young; I also think that the joy of raising tiny children can't fully be appreciated until they are big.

The stress of 'eighteen summers'

While I may have begun this chapter with sentimental, misty-eyed reminiscence, I'm also acutely aware that raising young people is not easy. I've said several times in this book that I believe in many ways it is harder than raising younger children and I stand by that, regardless of how much I talk about 'the lasts'. When we're trying to be mindful of letting go, I think we can also tend to put a huge amount of pressure on ourselves to 'enjoy every moment', which actually makes everything harder. As I said earlier, the idea that you 'only have eighteen summers with your children, so make them count' is well meant, but in reality, it creates stress for parents and carers who are just trying to survive one summer, especially one with bored young people.

And in any case, do we really only have eighteen summers? If we have worked hard at 'holding on' to our young people and have a good attachment with them, I'd hope that we would see many summers of shared fun. Maybe not every day, and maybe not a week or two on holiday, but if our young people feel respected and loved, they are going to want to spend time with us throughout their lives. The 'eighteen summers' idea completely misses this. So instead of heaping on the pressure to 'soak it all in' and 'always be present', I think better advice would be to realise that connection, attachment and unconditional love are lifelong.

Demetrescence – the last transition of a mother

Have you heard of the word 'matrescence'? Referring to the emotional and physical transition women go through when they become a mother, the term was coined by American anthropologist Dana Raphael in the 1970s. Raphael devoted her work to understanding and helping new mothers. She was a huge proponent of breastfeeding and was one of the earliest professionals to endorse the work of doulas – lay people who helped to support mothers-to-be, both physically and emotionally, through pregnancy, birth and postnatally. Although Raphael's work was hugely important and influential, it is only in recent years that the concept of matrescence has become popular, with multiple social media posts and several books and media articles devoted to it.

While I love the idea of matrescence, especially as somebody who worked as a doula for many years, I feel that it only explains half of the picture. Mothers do absolutely go through an important transition when they have a baby, but they also go through another huge transition when that baby grows into a teenager and later an adult. Yet there is no word to describe this process and very little is written about it.

I have pondered this many times and tried to come up with a name for this transition. Initially, I considered de-matrescence, with the idea that a mother has completed the process of matrescence and is now ready to move on to the next phase of her life, but the 'de' prefix makes it sound like a loss and too finite. I don't believe mothers ever stop growing and changing in response to their children, whether they're newborn or middle-aged. I kept coming back to the idea of growth, with the very earliest months and years being when you are sowing seeds and nurturing the seedlings into maturity. Indeed, when a parent or carer of a toddler asks me for discipline help and expresses concern that my methods aren't working because their toddler still tantrums, I will often reply with the Robert Louis Stevenson quote: 'Don't judge each day by the harvest you reap but by the seeds that you plant'. So if matrescence is the time to plough and prepare the earth for seed sowing and to gently water and nurture the seedlings, then with our young people we have begun to enter the era of harvesting, seeing the signs of our hard work begin to mature. I decided, therefore, to name this transition Demetrescence, after the Greek goddess of the harvest, Demeter – an idea that came to me during a family holiday in Crete, soaked in the history of the ancient gods and goddesses.

Demeter was one of the Olympian gods and goddesses. She was the daughter of Cronus (god of time) and Rhea (the mother goddess) and sister to Hestia (goddess of the home), Hera (goddess of women, family and marriage), Poseidon (god of the sea) and Zeus (god of the sky), to whom she was also a consort. Demeter was responsible for the growth of crops in spring and summer and for the harvest in autumn, and her legends revolve around her impact on agriculture in Ancient Greece.

Demeter's daughter, Persephone, was taken by Hades (god of the underworld) to be his wife. The loss of her daughter caused Demeter great distress, and she spent many months searching for her in vain, which was said to have caused a failed harvest and a great famine in Greece at the time. Demeter begged for Zeus's help (Zeus was father to Persephone), and he bargained with Hades to return her. Hades agreed, so long as Persephone had not eaten any fruit of the underworld, including the delicious pomegranates that grew there. Unfortunately, Persephone had already eaten from one, consuming six of its seeds. It was finally agreed that Persephone could return to Demeter, but only for six months of the year; the remaining six (one for every pomegranate seed she had eaten) she had to spend with Hades in the underworld. For the six months of the year that Persephone was with Demeter, seeds sprouted, flowers bloomed and crops grew and were harvested. When she returned to Hades the fields were barren, until the next spring and her return.

Demeter's love for Persephone, and the links to growth, harvest and letting go, albeit temporarily, make me think about the grieving-type processes that mothers go through as their children grow and go off out into the world alone. They know their children will return, and the love and connection are not severed, but they must also adjust to the process of having an empty nest, or a fallow field. Demetrescence I think perfectly describes this period of life, not just for mothers, but fathers, too. I would love one day for the concept of Demetrescence to receive as much attention as that of matrescence because both stages of life are transformational and equally as important and impactful on us.

When menopause and Demetrescence collide

Demetrescence is not the only life transition mothers of young people have to cope with. For those in their early to mid-forties, the perimenopause (the transition to full menopause) is also at play. Again, I do not think this is discussed enough.

In the last few years, menopause seems to have become a hot topic. You cannot pick up a newspaper, put on a current-affairs TV or radio show or venture on to middle-aged influencer accounts without hearing about the menopause or hormone replacement therapy (HRT). What is missing from all these con-versations, however, is the fact that women in this age group who are mothers are trying to balance the change in their bodies and the resulting changes in their brains brought on by chang-ing hormone levels, while also tackling the emotional impact of Demetrescence.

Both peri- and full menopause often bring with them big, difficult feelings. Some are caused by the changes in brain chem-istry that are a physical side effect, while others are caused by the emotions that accompany the realisation that you are leaving your fertility and youth behind you. This makes the thought of your young person growing up and becoming independent even more bittersweet, as you know the door will likely be closed on becoming pregnant again. That said, I know of many perimenopausal women who have welcomed 'surprise' babies or made the decision to try to add one more being to their family. This brings an even more confusing blend of transitions to the picture, as these mothers try to balance matrescence on the one hand with their new baby and Demetrescence on the other with their young people.

Once again, I don't have any sage advice here. Personally, I didn't experience a perimenopause – my menopause was in-duced medically when I was forty-three. One day I went to bed with entirely average oestrogen levels and a regular menstrual cycle, the next I woke up with no oestrogen, no periods and every single menopausal symptom you can imagine. Trying to cope with constant hot flushes and night sweats, as well as brain fog, insomnia and mood swings, while my young people were at the peak of their own big emotions and life challenges has at times felt insurmountable, but we've survived, with baby steps and a lot of 'rupture and repair'.

All I can add here is that you've survived every difficult day that you've had in your life so far and you will get through these big transitions, too. Be kind to yourself, be kind to your young person and lower your expectations of yourself. No parent can be perfect, especially not a perimenopausal or menopausal one.

What will you do now?

I remember in the run-up to my youngest child starting school marvelling at how much more time I would have for myself. I was self-employed and struggled to work with the limited hours of childcare I had. I had visions of ticking off my to-do list, emptying my email inbox and being able to take a nice, relaxing break for lunch each day. I even bought a couple of new books, imagining I would be able to get stuck into a chapter or two if I finished my work early, before the school pick-up rush began. Oh, how wrong I was. There was no free time, there were no leisurely lunches, just days spent trying to cram eight hours of work into the five and a half hours I had left between arriving home and leaving for the school run again. And I'll admit I had a few visions then of how wonderful it would be when my children had all grown up and left home and not only would I have genuinely free time, but my house would also stay spotless after I'd cleaned it.

What I didn't expect were the boredom and sense of emptiness that set in when my young people weren't around. In the two decades since I had last been on my own, I seemed to have forgotten who I was and what I liked doing. Demetrescence is all about reconnecting with your pre-child self. What did you used to enjoy that you have forgotten about or not had time for along the way? Perhaps you used to love playing team sports, learning new languages or singing in a choir? Now is the time to pick up those interests and hobbies again.

What else could you fill your heart, home and time with if you're concerned about having an empty nest? Now is a great time to consider the following:

- **A change in career** Is there something you always wished you had trained in but never did?
- **Volunteering** The volunteering I do really gives me a sense of purpose, and I love to know that I am giving back something to the community that helped me when my children were younger.
- **Studying** Taking evening classes or enrolling in an online course for no reason other than the enjoyment of learning is wonderfully empowering and confidence boosting.
- **Joining some local groups** Is there something you have an interest in but never explored? Floristry, beekeeping, bouldering, Nordic walking – you name it, there's a group for it somewhere! These are also great places to meet new friends, too.
- **Getting a dog** This is such a cliché, but so common. My rescue dog has definitely filled a hole left by my young people becoming increasingly independent.
- **Making a Demetrescence bucket list** Is there something crazy you've always wanted to try but never got around to or couldn't spare the money for? Make a bucket list of things you want to do and work to save up for the things on it. Just the act of saving gives you a goal and a sense of purpose.

You've given enough time to others – now it's finally time to give back to yourself. The possibilities are endless.

What to do if you struggle with Demetrescence

I think everybody struggles a little with the idea of their young people growing up and eventually leaving them. Of course, we're excited and we can also look forward to having more time to ourselves (and more money and a cleaner home, too!), but it is a tremendous transition. And just like matrescence, it's not a transition that happens quickly – I think it took me until my firstborn was around three or four years old before I began to feel properly competent as a parent.

We cannot expect to adjust to our young people's changing needs and the idea of letting go in just a few short weeks or months. The transition will take years, as we ourselves move from one stage of our lives to another, alongside our children. All transitions have bumpy periods. There are times that make us want to turn around and run back to the reassuring safety from which we started out. There are going to be wrong turns, dead ends and scary, dark alleyways before we reach our destination. Similarly, if we're on the journey with a travel mate, whether that's our spouse, partner or co-parent, there are going to be fallings-out and misunderstandings as we adjust to the inevitable changes in our adult relationships that occur as our own identities shift.

I think what I'm really saying here, is that there are no magic answers. Once again, there are no quick fixes to take away any trepidation or sadness. Life is about feeling all the feelings. Remember when we spoke about emodiversity and how important it is to embrace it with your young person? Well, the same is true for you, too. Don't be afraid to feel angry, sad, happy, anxious, excited, wistful and even jealous of the opportunities that lie ahead of your young person. Embrace the emodiversity that I've encouraged so much throughout this book, not only for your young person but for yourself, too. We spend so long focusing on our young people's emotions that we commonly dismiss our own, pushing them away to be dealt with another day. The key to Demetrescence is realising that that day is just around the corner, if it hasn't already arrived.

*

I hope this chapter has resonated with you and helped you to realise that what you're feeling now is common and normal. You're not alone. Millions of parents have trodden the path before you and millions will follow. 'Letting go' of your young person may feel like the end of an era, but really, it is just the beginning of a brand new one. There is so much to come for you, as well as your young person; enjoy the harvest – it's finally time to reap the rewards of all your hard work since you became a parent.

Let's move on now to our last chapter. This is the one for you if you have any niggling concerns remaining, as in it I answer the questions I am most commonly asked by parents and carers of young people.

Chapter 11

Raising Teens: FAQs

Kids need love the most when they're acting most unlovable.

ERMA BOMBECK, American humorist

Although I would love to have answered all your questions by this point in the book, I suspect there are a few niggles at the back of your mind. Whenever I write, I don't aim to be the 'all-knowing expert' because I don't feel that's empowering for you and, perhaps most importantly, I don't know you or your young person, or your unique circumstances. So while I have devoted this chapter to answering some of the most common questions I am asked by parents or carers of young people, please trust your instinct if you disagree with me, or my answer doesn't seem as if it will work for you and your family.

Frankly, there are no right or wrong answers in parenting, only what's right for you. I still often catch myself thinking, 'Gosh, I don't know what to do here?' so please don't chastise yourself too much (or blame me!) if you're still flummoxed by a situation after reading this book. We're all learning and growing every day and the expectations that we place upon ourselves to know the answers simply because we've been parents for quite some time now are ridiculously pointless and damaging. When all is said and done, I don't think you can go far wrong if you respond to an issue with empathy, respect and understanding for your young person.

Q. How do you get your young person to listen to you more?

A. I think the best place to start here is to try to remember what it was like to be a young person, when your parents or carers were constantly trying to get you to do certain things in certain ways, or indeed to not do something and you disagreed with them. Did you feel as if you had a voice? Did you feel that they respected you? Did you feel able to discuss the issue with them or reach a compromise, or was it very much their way or the highway? Why did you stop listening to them? What would have helped you to listen to them more?

It can often feel that we're nagging our young people because they simply do not listen to us. Then we end up going down a slippery path, where the more they feel nagged, the less likely they are to do what we've asked. When we become stressed, our communication is poor. We will often shout or become snappy, and nobody wants to listen to somebody who yells at them.

The key here is to work on your communication, stay calm and figure out, with your young person, how you can reach a compromise. Take time to listen to their concerns and suggestions with respect, so that they are more likely to return the favour with you. For instance, if you're asking them to pack their belongings away from the kitchen table, you may want them to do it 'right now', but they may be busy, or enjoying doing something else. Asking them when they think they will be able to do it and agreeing that as long as it's gone by the time you eat dinner is much more realistic.

Remember, if you want them to listen to you, you have to set a good example. If you find yourself constantly yelling, then the best way to get them to listen is to work on whatever you are carrying that is pushing you over the edge. Nobody wants to be yelled at; it's a guaranteed way to stop people listening to you.

Q. How can you stop your young person having a 'bad attitude'?

A. This is a question that I need a magic wand to answer. Alas, it is impossible.

Rewind to the very first chapter of this book when we were speaking about neurological development, emotion regulation, empathy and executive functions. Young people may look like us, they may be bigger than us and we often mistakenly believe that they are fully developed adults. Inside, however, their brains have a lot of work still to do. Young people are egocentric, their world rightly revolves around themselves because they are still developing their identities. They struggle with impulse control, they are more emotional than us in times of stress and they often say things they don't really mean because their lips engage quicker than the frontal cortex of their brain.

Adults often misinterpret all this normal adolescent develop-ment as 'attitude'. We mistakenly read rudeness and disrespect into young people's actions that just aren't there, or at least are not intended. Our young people's words or actions (I'm talking eye rolls, hand gestures, slamming doors and big huffs as they dramatically flounce out of the room) also trigger us, because we would have been in trouble if we had acted that way with our parents or carers. In those moments, we are transported back twenty years or thereabouts to when we were our young peo-ple's age. We were taught that adults should always be respected, otherwise there were consequences. Now, standing as the adults in the situation, our conditioning is screaming at us to yell at them, punish them, teach them a lesson, so that they know they cannot get away with speaking like that and showing such disrespect. We can break the cycle, though. We don't have to use the same discipline that we were raised with. Knowing more about young people's neurodevelopment we can choose to be understanding and accepting of the fact that their dysregulated emotions are no more than just that – emotions they are not yet fully in control of, and not 'attitude'.

Q. How do you make your young person tidy their bedroom?

A. This is a battle you are never going to win and, indeed, something that is not worth going into battle over. The best piece of advice I can give you here is to view your young person's bedroom as *their* domain, not yours. I know that it's in your home, which you pay for, but it is their space and therefore their decision as to how tidy it is.

Ground rules are important, though. You need to have boundaries about, say, storing an IKEA warehouseful of plates, glasses, mugs, cutlery and kitchen scissors (my young people's favourite hoarding object) in their bedroom. If your young person takes food or drink to their room, then they are expected to bring the dirty empties to the kitchen and wash them up or place them in the dishwasher once they've finished. Similarly, rubbish should go in a bin, not on the floor, and that bin should be emptied at least once a week. Wet towels should not be left to fester on the carpet, they should be hung up in the bathroom or put in the laundry basket and anything that needs washing (by them or by you, whatever your arrangements are) should also be put in the laundry basket, otherwise it won't get washed.

Outside of these rules, however, my advice is to take a deep breath when you walk past their room and shut the door so you can't see the mess. Your young person has to learn, by themselves, that life is much easier if they are organised, that precious things get broken when they are covered with a 'floordrobe' of discarded clothing and accidentally stepped on, and that homework, work passes and other important documents quickly get lost if they are discarded on the floor haphazardly. So long as they are not growing mould or hosting vermin in their room, leave them be.

Q. How do you stop your young person swearing?

A. Swearing, cursing, or whatever you call it, is really triggering to many adults. Many find it infuriating when their young people swear, and find it terribly embarrassing if they do so in public or in front of other family members.

I think this one is a personal decision. I myself enjoy swearing – not all words, but I do find a good curse works well for my stress levels now and again. Naturally, my young people also swear at times. I can't expect them to be better than me. So if it really bothers you, the first step to take here is to make sure that you, your partner, if you have one, and any close friends and family members that your young person mixes with stop swearing first.

If you decide it's not realistic to surround your young person with non-swearing role models, then it's time to have a conversation with them. Explain to them that many people are offended by swearing and it's important that they 'read the room' before they speak. If they are at school or work, then swearing is a definite no-no, too. Talk about being careful with their language around younger children, including their own siblings, if they have any, especially when out in public. I'm sure you've read posts in local Facebook groups in which a young parent complains about 'a group of uncouth teens swearing in front of little children in the park' and how teens today should 'have more respect'. While it's likely their little children will one day be the teens swearing, this thought isn't much consolation at the time. It's best, instead, that young people know that they should be mindful of their language in these situations.

Finally, I won't tolerate any language that is racist, sexist, ableist, homophobic or transphobic from my young people. A lot of slang swear words do tick these boxes, but often young people aren't aware of what they are saying, or of the roots of the words they are using. If you hear your young person using offensive words, then make sure you tell them to stop, and explain why. Without the explanation, they won't stop.

Q. How do you get your young people to help more around the house?

A. I think sometimes we're our own worst enemies here. When our young people were little and asked to help us, we would usually say, 'No, it's OK darling, thanks', and dismiss their offers because their 'help' was usually more of a hindrance. It was quicker for us to carry on working on the job alone. Unfortunately, these patterns tend to persist, until, one day, our children – or young people as they are now, stop offering their help. Obviously, you can't turn back the clock and change your response, embracing any help they offer, however much extra work it gives you. What you can do, though, is ask them for help.

Asking for help isn't something we're very good at. We tend to struggle with trying to get everything done ourselves, getting increasingly bitter about it. We curse our young people in our heads for not doing anything to help us (sometimes our partners, too, if we have one). We get angrier and angrier because they don't help out, until one day, we explode, often over something small, like an empty toilet roll left on the holder. This is a classic case of emotional displacement. The biggest problem here is that we presume our young people (and partners) are psychic. We presume they know that we're struggling and need help and we presume they know that we want them to do more. The thing is, they are so absorbed in their own worlds and thoughts that they simply do not pick up on our concerns. If we want their help, we have to tell them, with an emphasis on telling them, not yelling at them.

Next, we have to help our young people to understand exactly what we want them to do. Remember, they aren't great with rational-thinking skills, time management or organisation. Break down a task into individual steps – saying, for example, 'Please put this laundry basket full of clothing into the washing machine and turn it on to the thirty-degree setting. When it has finished, please hang it up to dry,' rather than simply, 'I need you to do the laundry'. The latter is far less likely to achieve the response you hope for.

Q. How do I get my young person to stick to their curfew?

A. Actually, a much better aim here is to explain to your young person why it's important that they contact you, as soon as possible, if they are going to be later than expected.

If we obsess about curfews and our young people are afraid of the punishment imposed if they miss them, they will learn to come up with convincing lies to try to avoid the consequences. I remember all sorts of fantastical tales my friends used to come up with when we were younger because their parents were strict and they would get into terrible trouble if they broke their curfews. On one occasion, we even pretended to be a school teacher, calling up to request that my friends stayed out late for a school concert rehearsal, while we hung out at the local park instead. Curfews didn't make them more responsible, but they did make them great liars.

If you are concerned about your young person's safety and whereabouts, it's much better to explain to them that 'more than anything else, I want to know that you're safe. Please text me with any updates if you are going somewhere different to what's planned, and if you are going to be later than xxx [whatever time you've agreed together], please call or text me and let me know your new estimated arrival time.' Over the years, my young people have become pretty good at this. They do forget sometimes, because as much as they know how important it is to me, their brains sometimes have other ideas, but a quick text from me prompting contact is usually enough for an update to follow.

If you want your young person to stay communicative with you, you have to give them a bit of trust and freedom. It's much more important to me that I know if my young people's plans change, than to have them scraping in one minute before an arbitrary curfew. For me, communication beats curfews every time.

Q. How do you tackle pocket money with teens?

A. I think pocket money is vital for teens, and yes, I do specifically mean teens here (because most young adults will either be in work or receiving student loans). Pocket money gives them some independence and can be a great tool to teach them how to budget (more on that in the next Q/A). It's also the best way I've found to navigate the constant requests to buy things that teens often make.

I have a few rules for pocket money. The first is that it is given unconditionally and is not related to behaviour, homework or chores. I give pocket money as a human right, not as a bribe – because we know that bribes are ineffective at changing behaviour in the long term and they just lead to requests for bigger rewards (or here, more money). The second is that the young person can choose how they want to spend the money – because once you give it to them, it is their money, not yours. The third is that I do not force them to save any of the money. Many parents and carers think making their young person save money teaches them good lessons for the future, but it doesn't. What they really need to learn a good lesson is to experience the natural consequences of having no money caused by a lack of saving. The fourth is that I do not lend money. If my young people want something that they cannot afford, then they need to save for it (this is what really inspires saving). Finally, we have rules concerning what the pocket money should and should not cover. In my family, I cover my young people's phones, toiletries, school uniform and any other school-related expenses, including travel and trips, classes and lessons, lunch money, and medical, dental and optical-related expenses. They are expected to pay for their clothing, social life and related travel costs, and anything else they want to buy. Aside from pocket money, I generally don't buy them anything not covered in the expenses list above, outside of Christmas and birthday presents.

How much you should give your young person for their pocket money is entirely down to you and your household budget. In the UK, the average monthly pocket money for teens is around £50–60, but obviously the amount you give should also consider what it is expected to cover.[1]

Q. How can you help your young person to manage their money better?

A. You can't make young people save or budget, but you can teach them how to do both. A good activity is to complete a simple budget planner. Print out a blank table, with two columns and at least ten rows. In the first column, they should make a list of everything they need, or want, to pay out for each month. Include any bills they pay themselves, like gym memberships, phone contracts, car insurance and so on, as well as entries for clothing and shoes, haircuts, make-up and skincare, lunch money, coffees/soft drinks, entertainment, petrol and so on. Then encourage your young person to complete it, making sure they enter a figure in each column. Once complete, they should tot up the figures, giving them their average monthly expenditure. They can take this further by splitting into 'essentials' and 'nice-to-haves'. Once they have completed the budget planner, they will also be able to calculate how much money they can save each month and decide on an amount to put away for things like car maintenance or saving towards a new phone. I think too often we expect young people to be able to budget, without fully explaining to them how to do so. Sometimes, it's only when everything is down in black and white that they can fully understand where their money goes.

If your young person runs out of money before their next pay day or pocket-money due date, try to resist lending them money. They may be desperate to go to the cinema with their friends, buy a pair of shoes in a sale or get a takeaway, but they have to learn that if they do not have the money, they simple cannot afford it and will need to wait. Lending them money may seem like the kind thing to do, but it isn't. It puts them into a 'buy-now' state of mind, which can lead to impulse buys and the chances of them getting into debt in the future. The only time I bail my young people out is if they run out of money and food (which isn't a rare occurrence if they're at university). If this happens, I send them an online shop with enough basics to get them through the week or two until their next loan instalment comes in. There are no treats or indulgences, but basic pasta, rice, bread, eggs, chopped tomatoes and the like, so they won't starve, but they won't feast either. I understand they struggle with impulse control and there's no point getting angry when the 'Mum-I'm-hungry-I-can't-afford-to-go-shopping' texts arrive, but they do need to learn. Of course, I will always help if I can, but there needs to be enough of an unpleasant consequence that they are motivated to budget better next time.

Q. How can you motivate your young person to get a job once they leave education?

A. Maybe your young person has just finished school or college or recently graduated and moved back home, spending their days in bed, online or moping around your living room, eating all your food. Understandably, you want them to get a job, to begin their career and start contributing towards the costs of the household budget. However, a lot of young people don't share these goals – not necessarily because they're lazy (as most are labelled in this scenario), but because they don't know where to start and don't have confidence in themselves to find a good job.

While schools, colleges and universities run careers events and practice CV-writing sessions, they tend to miss out the nitty- gritty of job hunting. Where should young people go to look for jobs? Do they understand what the different employment-related terms mean? What is temporary, contract, permanent? Full time, half time, flexi time? Freelance? Do they know where to search for an apprenticeship or traineeship? Do they know how to claim universal credit and book an appointment with a work coach if they're in the UK? Do they know how to register with an agency? Do they know how to write a cover letter? Do they have good inter-view skills? Do they have any idea what they want to do? All this can seem overwhelming, and the standard approach for a young person still working on their executive-function skills is to stick their head in the sand and do nothing. Taking time to sit with them and research the options together can help to spur them on.

If we, as parents and carers, constantly nag them and question when they are going to look for a job, we just add to the stress without doing anything to help them. As time goes on, young people can start to feel useless. Knowing that they should work but feeling stuck, their self-esteem nosedives and they become even less likely to step out of their comfort zone of staying home.

It's important here to emphasise to the young person that they are not necessarily making a decision for life. Entry-level jobs are usually just that – a first step on the career ladder – and their entire life path doesn't have to be mapped out at sixteen, eighteen or twenty-one. They have time to explore different industries and decide what suits them best. Lifting this pressure off can really help.

Finally, if they are struggling to find paid employment, you can encourage them to volunteer somewhere. This is a great way to build confidence and self-esteem and is an impressive addition to their CV, too.

Q. How do you encourage your young person to be anti-racist?

A. First up, don't presume that your young person fully understands racism. While we may pride ourselves on bringing our young people up to be inclusive, and believe that we have raised them not to be racist, it's likely that they still unconsciously are, especially if they are white. This doesn't mean that you've somehow failed; it just means that teaching young people not to be racist involves more than the superficial conversations many families have. If your young person (and indeed, you) don't fully understand the horrors that Black and brown people have gone through at the hands of white people in history, many in the not-so-distant past, then it's not possible for them to be anti-racist. If your young person is not aware of any unconscious biases they hold, then they are not anti-racist. Even if your young person has Black or brown friends, they can still be unconsciously racist. Even if they say, 'I don't see colour', they do – they may just not realise it yet.

You need to have the difficult conversations. You need to read about the truth of history that doesn't make it into the national curriculum, especially that relating to colonial heritage. Watch the documentaries together, encourage your young person to follow anti-racist influencers and buy books by Black and brown people explaining why most white people are still a long way from being truly anti-racist. You have to do this work, as well as your young person. It really is uncomfortable, especially when you realise that many of your efforts to be kind, gentle and inclusive when your young people were younger – buying them a brown doll and a book about Africa – were nowhere near enough.

As well as this, you need to pull your young person up on inappropriate use of offensive slang words, especially when they don't realise the racist connotations. Check your own language and that of your family members and friends. If it is racist, then pull them up on it, especially when your young person is with you. Finally, talk about racism with your young person often. Pick up on stories in the news with them, so that they see that racism is very much active today and not just a part of history. Becoming anti-racist is an ongoing journey, for you as well as your young person.

Q. What can you do if you think your young person's friends are a bad influence on them?

A. Your instincts are probably screaming at you to encourage your young person to ditch their friend, or group of friends, and to find somebody 'nicer'. Unfortunately, if you do this, it's unlikely to be received well by your young person and may very well push them more towards their friends and further away from you.

As hard as it is to watch your young person with somebody who seems to bring out the worst in them, this is something that they need to realise for themselves. If you are worried that your young person is getting into trouble, or you feel that the friendship is affecting their mental health, then you need to have a calm, honest conversation with them. But make it clear that you are not judging them or trying to make them ditch their friend; you just want to make sure that they know that friend-ships should be something that bring them joy, not sadness. It's more than likely that they will share the same opinion as you, given time, but reaching that place has to be something they do themselves. In the meantime, reiterate that you are always ready to listen to them if they need to chat. And if they do eventually leave the friendship, try to resist the urge to say, 'I told you so'.

Q. What do you do if you're worried about your young person's mental health?

A. The best advice I could give you here is, please, don't ever worry that you're being a nuisance or overdramatic. Reach out to a mental-health professional, your young person's form tutor, SENCO or pastoral lead at school or college, a support group or relevant charity. I am of the firm belief that it's better to be safe than sorry. Trust your instincts. If you feel that something is wrong, it usually is. Reach out to those who will really understand, who have been there, who can listen to you and support you. Take your worries seriously, and act on them.

Finally, I thought I would add a curveball of a question – one that's not strictly about your young person, but about you as a young person. And I'm including it because it's something I am commonly asked by parents and carers after I have discussed with them a lot of the information in this book. Perhaps it will resonate with you, too ...

Q. What can you do if this book has made you feel triggered about your own teen years?

A. Talking about treating your young person with empathy and respect and working together as a team to solve any problems can often be triggering for grown adults who were treated harshly by their own parents during their teen years. In order to be the best parents that we can be for our young people we have to make peace with our pasts. We have to revisit the times when we felt excluded, shamed, ignored, unsupported and emotionally hurt. Only when we learn to understand the effects of our own upbringings and the conditioning that we received from our own parents regarding how teenagers should behave and be treated can we can break free from the triggers that drive us towards unconscious, disrespectful behaviour towards our own young people.

This work isn't about making you feel angry at your own parents, and it isn't about souring your relationship with them. Remember, they too were teens once, and it's highly likely their own parents were even more unsupportive. They learned how to raise you from their own upbringing. But you have the chance now to break the cycle with your own young person. Unlike your parents, you are in the privileged position of having the information you need to make the change. Does this mean you have to forgive them, or forget how they made you feel? Definitely not. It's important to honour your feelings. But acting in a mind-minded way and considering the reasons why your parents said and did what they did is the starting point for de-activating your triggers and bringing more peace to your whole family.

I don't expect to have answered every question you have, but I hope that you can see the pattern in my approach for dealing with any issues relating to your young person. If you are struggling to solve your own conundrum, try to remember the following nine points:

- **Be mind-minded.** Consider how your young person is feeling and the underlying emotions that may be causing any difficult behaviour. Remember, no young person deliberately chooses to act in a difficult and dysregulated way.
- **Be emodiverse.** Embrace all emotions and let your young person know they are safe to be themselves with you. That doesn't mean you have to be their emotional punchbag. It's OK to have boundaries and to teach them calmer ways of expressing themselves.
- **Have realistic expectations.** If you expect your young person to behave like a mature adult, you're going to be disappointed. Many of the struggles faced by parents of young people arise because the parents, carers or teachers are expecting far too much of them.
- **Check their understanding.** Don't presume that your young person understands why something is important, or that they know how to do it. Check their understanding and provide explanations and instructions where needed.

- **Support your young person.** You need to be your young person's advocate and safe place. Use your adult brain and headspace to help 'hold' their big emotions and teach them to resolve issues, rather than try to punish them. You also need to be prepared to stand up for them when nobody else does.
- **Work collaboratively.** You and your young person are a team. It's the two of you (and other close family members) against the world, not you versus them. When you work together to solve problems, everything is easier.
- **Be a great role model.** No matter what you say, your young person is going to behave just like you, because your actions speak louder than your words. If you want them to be calm and respectful, then start by treating them that way first.
- **Repair the rupture.** If you don't quite manage to be a calm role model, just remember to apologise afterwards to heal the rupture. Your young person doesn't need you to be perfect, but they do need to know that you're human and that you make things right if you slip up.
- **Be the adult.** (More on this in my closing note on the next page.)

I hope that you have found this chapter useful, and as we near the end of the book, I hope that you feel more empowered to tackle any issues you have with your young person. Most importantly, I hope that you understand them a little more now, and perhaps yourself and your own upbringing, too.

If ever you have a time when you're not sure what you should do, shut out the noise, focus on your instincts, trust yourself and trust your young person and you can't go far wrong.

A Brief Closing Note

And so we come to the end of the book. We've travelled full circle, from holding on to letting go, and at the centre of everything we have discussed is us. So many of us want to try to change our young people, when what we really need to do is to change ourselves.

We need to understand ourselves and everything we bring to parenting – some good things, some not so good. To raise the happiest, emotionally healthiest teens and young adults, we have to start with our own thoughts, feelings, understanding and actions. Repeatedly throughout this book I have referred to you needing to 'be the adult'. And in the times when you have had enough, when you feel that you just can't cope with your young person any more and everything inside of you is screaming at you to yell, punish, shame and scare your young person into submission, that's when you need to be the adult the most. Your young person needs you to bring your emotional maturity and regulation to the table, not join them in their dysregulation.

So before we finish, I'd like to leave you with an acronym to help you remember to 'be the adult' – because honestly, if you remember nothing else from this book, being the adult is enough to make a huge change in your relationship with your young person, which, in turn, will reflect positively on their behaviour.

Be the adult

Believe in them, especially when nobody else does.
Encourage them, but don't push.

Tame your own emotions, so you can help them to tame theirs.
Heal triggers from your past, so you are not repeating cycles of harsh discipline.
Empathise with them – because understanding their feelings changes everything.

Awareness of attachment and its importance, to remind you that connection is key.
Developmental awareness, with realistic expectations of your young person.
Unconditional love, the foundation of Maslow's pyramid.
Listen to them; remember: 'two ears, one mouth'.
Trustworthy and reliable – if you want your young person to act this way, you have to model it.

Finally, I'd like to quickly ask you now to go right back to the start of the book and the notes you made based on my questions in the Introduction, when I asked you to imagine yourself as a teenager, struggling with your behaviour or a tricky situation where you felt misunderstood:

- What was happening at that time in your world?
- How were you feeling?
- How were you behaving?
- What did you hope your parents or carers would say to you?
- What did they actually say or do?

Reflecting on these answers now, I hope you realise that right from the beginning of this book you already had the answers – you are already your own expert and you know your own young person far better than I (or any other author or expert) do.

The secret to raising a teen or young adult is not really so secret, and it's certainly not complicated. It's simply being the person you needed when you were their age.

Resources

Sarah Ockwell-Smith's social media

- Facebook: www.facebook.com/sarahockwellsmithauthor
- Instagram: www.instagram.com/sarahockwellsmith
- YouTube: www.youtube.com/c/sarahockwellsmith
- TikTok: www.tiktok.com/sarahockwellsmith
- Website: www.sarahockwell-smith.com
- Sarah's 'Gentle Parenting Tweens and Teens' discussion group: www.facebook.com/groups/gentleparentingtweensteens

Other relevant books by Sarah Ockwell-Smith

- *How to be a Calm Parent: Lose the guilt, control your anger, and tame the stress – for more peaceful and enjoyable parenting and calmer, happier children too*, Piatkus, 2021
- *Because I Said So! Why society is childist and how breaking the cycle of discrimination towards children can change the world*, Piatkus, 2023

Adolescent mental health

- Young Minds: www.youngminds.org.uk
- Mind: www.mind.org.uk

- Beyond: www.wearebeyond.org.uk
- Nightline: www.nightline.ac.uk
- Student Minds: www.studentminds.org.uk

ADHD support

- ADHD UK: www.adhduk.co.uk
- ADHD Foundation: www.adhdfoundation.org.uk

Alcohol and young people

- Drinkaware: www.drinkaware.co.uk

Autism support

- National Autistic Society: www.autism.org.uk
- BeyondAutism: www.beyondautism.org.uk

Anxiety support

- Anxiety UK: www.anxietyuk.org.uk

Apprenticeships

- Gov.uk: https://www.gov.uk/apply-apprenticeship

Bullying support

- Ditch the Label: www.ditchthelabel.org
- National Bullying Helpline:
  www.nationalbullyinghelpline.co.uk
- Anti-Bullying Alliance: www.anti-bullyingalliance.org.uk

Drugs and young people

- Frank: www.talktofrank.com
- Narcotics Anonymous: www.ukna.org

Eating disorders support

- Beat: www.beateatingdisorders.org.uk

EBSA support

- Not Fine in School: www.notfineinschool.co.uk

Online safety information

- Childnet: www.childnet.com
- eSafety Training: www.esafetytraining.org
- Internet Matters: www.internetmatters.org
- UK Safer Internet Centre: www.saferinternet.org.uk

SEND support

- IPSEA: www.ipsea.org.uk
- Family Action: www.family-action.org.uk

Suicide prevention

- Papyrus: www.papyrus-uk.org
- Maytree: www.maytree.org.uk

Teen pregnancy support

- British Pregnancy Advisory Service: www.bpas.org

- Brook: www.brook.org.uk
- Life Charity: www.lifecharity.org.uk

References

Chapter 1

1 Dubois-Comtois, K., Cyr, C., Pascuzzo, K., et al. (2013), 'Attachment theory in clinical work with adolescents', *Journal of Child and Adolescent Behavior*, 1: 111.

2 Doyle, A. B., Moretti, M. M., Ottawa: Health Canada, Child, and Family Division (2000), 'Attachment to parents and adjustment in adolescence: Literature review and policy implications'.

3 Mónaco, E., Schoeps, K. and Montoya-Castilla, I. (2019), 'Attachment syles and wellbeing in adolescents: How does emotional development affect this relationship?', *International Journal of Environmental Research and Public Health*, 17 July; 16(14): 2554.

4 Bostik, K. E. and Everall, R. D. (2007), 'Healing from suicide: Adolescent perceptions of attachment relationships', *British Journal of Guidance and Counselling*, 35: 79–96.

5 Gamble, S. A. and Roberts, J. E. (2005), 'Adolescents' perceptions of primary caregivers and cognitive style: The roles of attachment security and gender', *Cognitive Therapy and Research*, 29, 123–41.

6 American Time Use Survey, https://ourworldindata.org/time-with-others-lifetime – accessed online 16 November 2023.

Chapter 2

1 Peper, J. and Dahl, R. (2013), 'Surging hormones: Brain–behavior interactions during puberty', *Current Directions in Psychological Science*, April; 22(2): 134–9.

2 Op de Macks, Z. A., Bunge, S. A., Bell, O. N., et al. (2016),

'Risky decision-making in adolescent girls: The role of pubertal hormones and reward circuitry', *Psychoneuroendocrinology*, December; 74: 77–91.

3   Roenneberg, T., Kuehnle, T., Pramstaller, P. P., et al. (2004), 'A marker for the end of adolescence', *Current Biology*, 14: 1038–9.

4   Arain, M., Haque, M., Johal, L., et al. (2013), 'Maturation of the adolescent brain', *Neuropsychiatric Disease and Treatment*, 9: 449–61.

5   Dumontheil, I. (2014), 'Development of abstract thinking during childhood and adolescence: The role of rostrolateral prefrontal cortex', *Developmental Cognitive Neuroscience*, 10: 57–76.

6   Schreuders, E., Braams, B. R., Blankenstein, N. E., et al. (2018), 'Contributions of reward sensitivity to ventral striatum activity across adolescence and early adulthood', *Childhood Development*, May; 89(3): 797–810.

7   Chein, J., Albert, D., O'Brien, L., et al. (2011), 'Peers increase adolescent risk taking by enhancing activity in the brain's reward circuitry', *Developmental Science*, March; 14(2): F1–10.

8   Valle, A., Massaro, D., Castelli, I., et al. (2015), 'Theory of mind development in adolescence and early adulthood: The growing complexity of recursive thinking ability', *European Journal of Psychology*, 27 February; 11(1): 112–24.

9   Lorenz-Spreen, P., Mønsted, B. M., Hövel, P., et al. (2019), 'Accelerating dynamics of collective attention', *Nature Communications*, 10: 1759.

10   O'Nions, E., Peterson, I., Buckman, J., et al. (2018), 'Autism in England: Assessing underdiagnosis in a population-based cohort study of prospectively collected primary care data', *Lancet*, 29.

11   Sayal, K., Prasad, V., Daley, D., et al. (2018), 'ADHD in children and young people: Prevalence, care pathways, and service provision', *Lancet Psychiatry*, 5(2): 175–86.

12   Hosozawa, M., Sacker, A., Mandy, W., et al. (2020), 'Determinants of an autism spectrum disorder diagnosis in childhood and adolescence: Evidence from the UK Millennium Cohort Study', *Autism*, 24(6): 1557–65.

13   Russell, G., Stapley, S., Newlove-Delgado, T., et al. (2022), 'Time trends in autism diagnosis over 20 years: A UK population-based cohort study', *Journal of Child Psychology and Psychiatry*, 63(6): 674–82.

Chapter 3

1 Maslow, A. H. (1943), 'A theory of human motivation', *Psychological Review*, 50(4): 370–96.

2 Baumeister, R. and Leary, M. (1995), 'The need to belong: Desire for interpersonal attachments as a fundamental human motivation', *Psychological Bulletin*, 117: 497–529.

3 Goebel, B. L. and Brown, D. R. (1981), 'Age differences in motivation related to Maslow's need hierarchy', *Developmental Psychology*, 17(6): 809–15.

4 O'Brien, K. and Bowles, T. (2013), 'The importance of belonging for adolescents in secondary school settings', *European Journal of Social and Behavioural Sciences*, 5(2); ISSN 2301–2218 (online).

5 Fabris, M. A., Settanni, M., Longobardi, C., et al. (2023), 'Sense of belonging at school and on social media in adolescence: Associations with educational achievement and psychosocial maladjustment', *Child Psychiatry and Human Development*, 15 March.

6 Dwairy, M. (2010), 'Parental acceptance–rejection: A fourth cross-cultural research on parenting and psychological adjustment of children', *Journal of Child and Family Studies*, 19: 30–5.

7 Lorijn, S. J., Engels, M. C., Huisman, M., et al. (2022), 'Long-term effects of acceptance and rejection by parents and peers on educational attainment: A study from pre-adolescence to early adulthood', *Journal of Youth and Adolescence*, 51: 540–55.

8 Erikson, E. H. (1994), *Identity and the Life Cycle*. New York, NY: W. W. Norton.

9 Marcia, J. E. (1966), 'Development and validation of ego-identity status', *Journal of Personality and Social Psychology*, 3(5): 551–8.

10 Meeus, W., Van de Schoot, R., Keijsers, L., et al. (2012), 'Identity statuses as developmental trajectories: A five-wave longitudinal study in early-to-middle and middle-to-late adolescents', *Journal of Youth and Adolescence*, August; 41(8): 1008–21.

11 Elkind, D. (1967), 'Egocentrism in adolescence', *Child Development*, 38(4): 1025–34.

12 Census 2021: Gender identity: Age and sex, England and Wales.

13 Van der Miesen, A., Cohen-Kettenis, P. T. and De Vries, A. (2018), 'Is there a link between gender dysphoria and autism spectrum disorder?' *Journal of the American Academy of Child and Adolescent Psychiatry*, November; 57(11): 884–5.

14   Karrington, B. (2022), 'Defining desistance: Exploring desistance in transgender and gender expansive youth through systematic literature review', *Transgender Health*, 13 June; 7(3): 189–212.

15   Kamiya, M. (1980), *On the Meaning of Life*. Japan: Misuzu Shobo.

16   Miralles, F. and Garcia, H. (2017) *Ikigai: The Japanese Secret to a Long and Happy Life*. London: Penguin Life.

17   Ishida, R. (2012), 'Purpose in life (ikigai), a frontal lobe function, is a natural and mentally healthy way to cope with stress', *Psychology*, 3.

Chapter 4

1   *Cambridge Dictionary*, https://dictionary.cambridge.org/dictionary/english/confidence – accessed online 14 November 2023.

2   Newlove-Delgado, T., Marcheselli, F., Williams, T., et al. (2022), 'Mental health of children and young people in England', NHS Digital, Leeds.

3   Frenkel, E., Kugelmass, S. and Nathan, M. (1995), 'Locus of control and mental health in adolescence and adulthood', *Schizophrenia Bulletin*, 21(2): 219–26.

4   Costatini, I., Kwong, A., Smith, D., et al. (2021), 'Locus of control and negative cognitive styles in adolescence as risk factors for depression onset in young adulthood: Findings from a prospective birth cohort study', *Frontiers in Psychology*, 25 March; 12: 599240.

5   Felicia, F., Satiadarma, M. and Subroto, U. (2022), 'The relationship between locus of control and resilience in adolescents whose parents are divorced', 3rd Tarumanagara International Conference on the Applications of Social Sciences and Humanities.

6   Department for Work and Pensions (2023), 'Households below average income: Statistics on the number and percentage of people living in low-income households for financial years 1994/95 to 2021/22', Table 1.4a.

7   Quoidbach, G., Mikolajczak, M., et al. (2014), 'Emodiversity and the emotional ecosystem', *Journal of Experimental Psychology: General*, 143(6): 2057–66.

8   Heshmati, S., DavyRomano, E., Chow, C., et al. (2023), 'Negative emodiversity is associated with emotional eating in adolescents: An examination of emotion dynamics in daily life', *Journal of Adolescence*, January; 95(1): 115–30.

9   Hughes, C., Aldercotte, A. and Foley, S. (2017), 'Maternal mind-mindedness provides a buffer for pre-adolescents at risk for disruptive behavior', *Journal of Abnormal Child Psychology*, February; 45(2): 225–35.
10 Office for National Statistics (ONS) (2022), 'Suicides in England and Wales: 2021 registrations', ONS Statistical Bulletin, 6 September (online).
11 Markey, C. N. (2010), 'Invited commentary: Why body image is important to adolescent development', *Journal of Youth and Adolescence*, 39: 1387–91.
12 Lowe, M. R., Annunziato, R. A., Markowitz, J., et al. (2006), 'Multiple types of dieting prospectively predict weight gain during the freshman year of college', *Appetite*, 47(1): 83–90.
13 Wertheim, E., Mee, V. and Paxton, S. (1999), 'Relationships among adolescent girls' eating behaviors and their parents' weight-related attitudes and behaviors', *Sex Roles*, 41: 169–87.
14 Haines, J., Neumark-Sztainer, D., Hannan, P., et al. (2008), 'Child versus parent report of parental influences on children's weight-related attitudes and behaviors', *Journal of Pediatric Psychology*, 33(7): 783–8.
15 Iwamoto, D. K., Brady, J., Kaya, A., et al. (2018), 'Masculinity and depression: A longitudinal investigation of multidimensional masculine norms among college men', *American Journal of Men's Health*, November; 12(6): 1873–81.

Chapter 5

1   King's College London Policy Institute (2023), 'Parenting priorities: International attitudes to raising children', The World Values Survey.
2   Suárez-Relinque, C., Del Moral Arroyo, G., León-Moreno, C., et al. (2019), 'Child-to-parent violence: Which parenting style is more protective? A study with Spanish adolescents', *International Journal of Environmental Research and Public Health*, 12 April; 16(8): 1320.
3   Arım, R. G., Dahinten, V. S., Marshall, S. K., et al. (2011), 'An examination of the reciprocal relationships between adolescents' aggressive behaviors and their perceptions of parental nurturance', *Journal of Youth and Adolescence*, February; 40(2): 207–20.
4   Zubizarreta, A., Calvete, E., Hankin, B. L. (2019), 'Punitive parenting style and psychological problems in childhood: The

moderating role of warmth and temperament', *Journal of Child and Family Studies*, 28: 233–44.

5 Galván, A. (2013), 'The teenage brain: Sensitivity to rewards', *Current Directions in Psychological Science*, 22(2): 88–93.

6 Center for Disease Control and Prevention (2021), Youth Risk Behavior Survey.

Chapter 6

1 Richard Branson Virgin blog, https://www.virgin.com/branson-family/richard-branson-blog/my-message-to-anyone-disheartened-by-exam-results – accessed online 23 November 2023.

2 Fernández-Alonso, R., Álvarez-Díaz, M., Suárez-Álvarez, J., et al. (2017), 'Students' achievement and homework assignment strategies', *Frontiers in Psychology*, 7 March; 8: 286.

3 Walker, J., Hoover-Dempsey, K., Whetselm, D., et al. (2004), 'Parental involvement in homework: A review of current research and its implications for teachers, after school program staff, and parent leaders', Cambridge, MA: Harvard Family Research Project; Harvard Graduate School of Education.

4 Núñez, J. C., Epstein, J. L., Suárez, N., et al. (2017), 'How do student prior achievement and homework behaviors relate to perceived parental involvement in homework?' *Frontiers in Psychology*, 27 July; 8: 1217.

5 Equality Act 2010, www.legislation.gov.uk/ukpga/2010/15/contents – accessed online 23 November 2023.

6 Gov.UK (2018), 'Longitudinal study of young people in England', cohort 2, wave 2.

7 Ladd, G. W., Ettekal, I. and Kochenderfer-Ladd, B. (2017), 'Peer victimization trajectories from kindergarten through high school: Differential pathways for children's school engagement and achievement?' *Journal of Educational Psychology*, 109(6): 826–41.

8 Halterbeck, M., Conlon, G., Patrignani, P. and Pritchard, A. (2020), *Lost Learning, Lost Earnings*. London: The Sutton Trust.

9 Gov.UK (2023), 'Pupil absence in schools in England: Autumn and spring term 2022/23'.

10 Widome, R., Berger, A. T., Iber, C., et al. (2020), 'Association of delaying school start time with sleep duration, timing, and quality among adolescents', *JAMA Pediatrics*, 1 July; 174(7): 697–704.

11 Gradisar, M., Gardner, G. and Dohnt, H. (2011), 'Recent worldwide sleep patterns and problems during adolescence: A review and meta-analysis of age, region, and sleep', *Sleep Medicine*, February; 12(2): 110–118.

12 Wolfson, A. R. and Carskadon, M. A. (1998), 'Sleep schedules and daytime functioning in adolescents', *Child Development*, August; 69(4): 875–7.

13 Short, M. A., Blunden, S., Rigney, G., et al. (2018), 'Cognition and objectively measured sleep duration in children: A systematic review and meta-analysis', *Sleep Health*, June; 4(3): 292–300.

14 Spruyt, K., Molfese, D. L. and Gozal, D. (2011), 'Sleep duration, sleep regularity, body weight, and metabolic homeostasis in school-aged children', *Pediatrics*, February; 127(2): e345–52.

15 Czeisler, C. A., Kronauer, R. E., Allan, J. S., et al. (1989), 'Bright light induction of strong (type 0) resetting of the human circadian pacemaker', *Science*, 16 June; 244(4910): 1328–33.

16 Fan, X., Liao, C., Matsuo, K., et al. (2023), 'A single-blind field intervention study of whether increased bedroom ventilation improves sleep quality', *Science of the Total Environment*, 1 August; 884: 163805.

17 Baradaran Mahdavi, S., Mansourian, M., Shams, E., et al. (2020), 'Association of sunlight exposure with sleep hours in Iranian children and adolescents: The CASPIAN-V Study', *Journal of Tropical Pediatrics*, 1 February; 66(1): 4–14.

18 Kim, D. H., Kim, B., Lee, S. G., et al. (2023), 'Poor sleep is associated with energy drink consumption among Korean adolescents', *Public Health Nutrition*, December; 26(12): 3256–65.

19 Tomanic, M., Paunovic, K., Lackovic, M., et al. (2022), 'Energy drinks and sleep among adolescents', *Nutrients*, 15 September; 14(18): 3813.

20 Gardiner, C., Weakley, J., Burke, L. M., et al. (2023), 'The effect of caffeine on subsequent sleep: A systematic review and meta-analysis', *Sleep Medicine Review*, June; 69: 101764.

21 Kallappa, C. and Ninan, T. (2015), 'Excessive daytime sleepiness in teenagers – could it be due to iron deficiency?' *Archives of Disease in Childhood*; 100: A144.

Chapter 7

1 Adachi, P. J. and Willoughby, T. (2013), 'More than just fun and games: The longitudinal relationships between strategic video

games, self-reported problem-solving skills, and academic grades', *Journal of Youth and Adolescence*, 42: 1041–52.

2 Anderson, C. A., Shibuya, A., Ihori, N., et al. (2010), 'Violent video game effects on aggression, empathy, and prosocial behavior in Eastern and Western countries: A meta-analytic review', *Psychological Bulletin*, 136: 151–73.

3 O'Reilly, M., Dogra, N., Hughes, J., et al. (2019), 'Potential of social media in promoting mental health in adolescents', *Health Promotion International*, 1 October; 34(5): 981–91.

4 O'Reilly, M., Dogra, N., Whiteman, N., et al. (2018), 'Is social media bad for mental health and wellbeing? Exploring the perspectives of adolescents', *Clinical Child Psychology and Psychiatry*, October; 23(4): 601–13.

5 NHS UK (2022), 'Mental health of children and young people in England, follow up to the 2017 survey', online report.

6 NHS Digital (2019), 'Smoking, drinking and drug use among young people in England 2018', online report.

7 Public Health England (2022), 'Hospital Episode Statistics (HES) – mid year population estimates', online report.

8 Marshall, E. (2014), 'Adolescent alcohol use: Risks and consequences', *Alcohol and Alcoholism*, 49(2): 160–4.

9 Skogen, J. C., Sivertsen, B., Lundervold, A. J., et al. (2014), 'Alcohol and drug use among adolescents: And the co-occurrence of mental health problems, a population-based study', *BMJ Open*, 22 September; 4(9): e005357.

10 Boden, M. and Day, E. (2023), 'Illicit drug use in university students in the UK and Ireland: A PRISMA-guided scoping review', *Substance Abuse and Treatment Prevention Policy*, 14 March; 18(1): 18.

11 Action on Smoking and Health (2023), 'Use of e-cigarettes (vapes) among young people in Great Britain', ASH factsheet, June.

12 Yuan, M., Cross, S. J., Loughlin, S. E., et al. (2015), 'Nicotine, and the adolescent brain', *Journal of Physiology*, 15 August; 593(16): 3397–412.

13 Rubinstein, M. L., Delucchi, K., Benowitz, N. L., et al. (2018), 'Adolescent exposure to toxic volatile organic chemicals from e-cigarettes', *Pediatrics*, 141(4): e20173557.

14 Khambayat, S., Jaiswal, A., Prasad, R., et al. (2023), 'Vaping among adolescents: An overview of e-cigarette use in middle and high school students in India', *Cureus*, 13 May 15(5): e38972.

15 Lopez-Quintero, C., Hasin, D. S., De los Cobos, J. P., et

al. (2011), 'Probability and predictors of remission from life-time nicotine, alcohol, cannabis, or cocaine dependence: results from the National Epidemiologic Survey on Alcohol and Related Conditions', *Addiction*, 106(3): 657–69.

16 Tsai, J., Walton, K., Coleman, B. N., et al. (2018), 'Reasons for electronic cigarette use among middle and high school students – National Youth Tobacco Survey, United States', *Morbidity and Mortality Weekly Report*, 67(6): 196–200.

Chapter 8

1 Alsarrani, A., Hunter, R. F., Dunne, L., et al. (2022), 'Association between friendship quality and subjective wellbeing among adolescents: A systematic review', *BMC Public Health*, 22: 2420.

2 Van Harmelen, A.-L., Kievit, R., Ioannidis, K., et al. (2017), 'Adolescent friendships predict later resilient functioning across psychosocial domains in a healthy community cohort', *Psychological Medicine*, 47(13): 2312–22.

3 Kiesner, J., Kerr, M. and Stattin, H. (2004), 'Very important persons in adolescence: Going beyond in-school, single friendships in the study of peer homophily', *Journal of Adolescence*, 27(5): 545–60.

4 Pew Research Center (2018), 'Teens and tech survey dataset', online report.

5 Currie, D. H., Kelly, D. M. and Pomerantz, S. (2007), '"The power to squash people": Understanding girls' relational aggression', *British Journal of Sociology of Education*, 28(1): 23–37.

6 Girlguiding (2016), 'Girls' attitude survey'.

7 *Independent* (2019), 'Study charts the age you're most likely to experience major life events', https://www.independent.co.uk/life-style/health-and-families/life-events-age-study-marriage-first-home-poll-revealed-a8958996.html – accessed online 29 November 2023.

8 Suleiman, A. B. and Harden, K. P. (2016), 'The importance of sexual and romantic development in understanding the developmental neuroscience of adolescence', *Developmental Cognitive Neuroscience*, 17: 145–7.

9 Fortin, A., Fortin, L. and Paradis, A. (2022), 'Relationship quality among dating adolescents: Development and validation of the Relationship Quality Inventory for Adolescents', *Frontiers in Psychology*, 13.

10 Kelly, Y., Zilanawala, A., Tanton, C., et al. (2019), 'Partnered

intimate activities in early adolescence: Findings from the UK Millennium Cohort Study', *Journal of Adolescent Health*, September; 65(3): 397–404.

11   Geary, R. S., Tomes, C., Jones, K. G., et al. (2016), 'Actual and preferred contraceptive sources among young people: Findings from the British National Survey of Sexual Attitudes and Lifestyles', *BMJ Open*, 6: e011966.

12   Office for National Statistics (2023), 'Conceptions in England and Wales in 2021'.

13   Common Sense Media (2022), 'Teens and pornography report', https://www.commonsensemedia.org/sites/default/files/ research/report/2022-teens-and-pornography-final-web.pdf – accessed online 29 November 2023.

14   Strassberg, D., Rullo, J., Mackaronis, J. (2014), 'The sending and receiving of sexually explicit cell phone photos ("sexting") while in high school: One college's students' retrospective reports', *Computers in Human Behavior*, 41: 177–83.

15   Trill Mag (2022), 'Andrew Tate's chokehold on young lost men', https://www.trillmag.com/life/social-media/andrew-tates-chokehold-on-young-lost-men%EF%BF%BC/ – accessed online 29 November 2023.

16   UK Census (2020), 'Sexual orientation', https://www.ons. gov.uk/peoplepopulationandcommunity/culturalidentity/ sexuality/bulletins/sexualidentityuk/2020 – accessed online 29 November 2023.

17   Lenhart, A., Smith, A. and Anderson, M. (2015), 'Teens, technology and romantic relationships', Pew Research Center, http://assets.pewresearch.org/wp-content/ uploads/sites/9/2015/10/PI_2015-10-01_teens-technology-romance_FINAL.pdf – accessed online 29 November 2023.

18   The Trevor Project (2019), The Trevor Project research brief: Diversity of youth sexual orientation. Available at: https:// www.thetrevorproject.org/wp-content/uploads/2021/08/ Trevor-Project-Sexual-Orientation-Research-Brief_September. pdf – accessed online 29 November 2023.

19   Gleason, T. R., Theran S. A. and Newberg, E. M. (2017), 'Parasocial interactions and relationships in early adolescence', *Frontiers in Psychology*, 23 February; 8:255.

20   Ibid.

Chapter 11

1 Statista (2022), 'Average value of pocket money per week in the United Kingdom (UK) as of 2021, by age', online report.

Index